GET IN THE ARK

GET IN THE ARK

Steve Farrar

THOMAS NELSON PUBLISHERS®
Nashville

ISBN 0-7852-7310-7

Printed in the United States of America

1 2 3 4 5 6 QWV 05 04 03 02 01 00

To Doctor Dean Gage

Fellow worker,

Fellow soldier,

Trusted friend.

CONTENTS

1

GROUND ZERO

The most extraordinary thing about human beings is that they pursue ends which they know to be disastrous and turn their backs on ways which they know to be joyous.

—Malcolm Muggeridge

THE OLD TESTAMENT prophets never took any polls. They simply listened to the Spirit of God and declared His message.

Men like Isaiah, Jeremiah, and Habakkuk (just to mention a few) had a very clear message: Judgment was on its way.

A close examination of their inspired writings points to the fact that their message is of particular relevance to our day.

Throughout biblical history to the present time, God has dealt with His people in the same way. God has blessed His people. Time and again they have forgotten Him, turned their hearts from Him, and denied Him. Time and again they have slid down the slippery slope from compromise to all-out immorality and debauchery. And

1

time and again, at a particular point of no return, they have incurred the judgment of God.

We never seem to learn.

Why should we think that America will be different?

The signs are all there. America has been blessed by God. We have had more blessings than any nation in history. But we have forgotten Him, turned away from Him, and denied Him. We have crossed one line after another until we have found ourselves sliding down the greased incline toward destruction. Some say that America is "slouching toward Gomorrah." But when we study Scripture it becomes clear that we are not slouching. We are at Gomorrah's door! Scripture tells us that America is ripe for judgment. In fact, we are *more* than ripe: We are overdue.

Some will immediately assume that this book is about the return of Christ. It is not. I do not equate the coming judgment on our nation with Christ's second coming. Christ may return in five days, or He may not return for five hundred years. Yes, there are indicators that His coming could be near, but that is not the focus of this book. The subject at hand is God's judgment on a nation that has gone after other gods.

For the past year I have preached this message around the United States. I have found that Christians everywhere are beginning to sense the same thing. They know that something is out of kilter, that something is deeply wrong. And they are keenly aware that we cannot continue going down this road without severe consequences. At the same time godly Christian leaders have begun to speak up, men who are not given to extremism or sensationalism.

Several months ago I spoke on the subject of coming judgment at a conference center in North Carolina. A few weeks later Henry Blackaby, whose book *Experiencing God* has had a profound impact, was speaking there. In the question-answer session that followed, someone asked him:

"Dr. Blackaby, what do you see as the future for the United States?"

A friend faxed me his stunning reply, which was four pages in length. Let me give you a portion of what he had to say:

If you put the United States up against the Scriptures, we're in trouble. I think we're very close to the judgment of God.

The problem with America is not the unbelieving world. The problem with America is the people of God. You see, right now there are just as many divorces in the churches as outside the churches. There are just as many abortions inside the churches as outside the churches. There's only a one-percent difference in gambling inside the churches than outside the churches. George Barna did a survey of 152 separate items comparing the lost world and the churches, and he said there's virtually no difference between the two.

Our gospel is cancelled by the way we live. I'm never surprised at what the world does. The problem's with the light. The light no longer dispenses the darkness. And all the way through the Bible, the judgment came on a nation when God's people would not return unto Him.

In his book *America's Last Call*—you ought to read it, it's very powerful—David Wilkerson says the sin of America has outdone every other generation, including Noah's day, Sodom and Gomorrah, and any other time in history. The combination and extensiveness of the sin of America outdoes them all. Do we then suppose God is going to spare us judgment? I don't believe so. As a matter of fact, the greater the knowledge, the greater the judgment. We've had greater knowledge about God than any other generation in history, yet we're doing as little about it as possible. So I am very fearful about judgment.

You just need to know that my heart is very, very heavy about the day in which we live.

I hope if you didn't hear anything else that comes from this conference, that you will understand that it's God's people who hold the destiny of America. Don't fuss at the world. It's acting just like its nature. God's attention is focused on His own people. The future of America rests in our hands.[1]

In a recent newsletter, Dr. James Dobson printed a portion of Blackaby's words, and then commented, "Sadly, I believe Dr. Blackaby's assessment of America is entirely accurate . . . If revival is to occur, it will begin within the household of faith, and if not there, then judgment on this nation is likely."[2]

I agree with Dr. Dobson. Blackaby is right on the money.

There is a growing consensus throughout the body of Christ. America is in serious trouble. We have reached the point of no return. And, short of a divine miracle, judgment is inevitable—such a judgment as you and I have not witnessed in our lifetimes.

But don't take my word or anyone else's word for it. Look into the Scriptures and decide for yourself. Is judgment coming? That's a question we must answer in the light of God's Word.

But there is also a second part to the message of this book.

Yes, God judges evil nations. But in the midst of judgment, *God always has His remnant.*

Who are people who make up the remnant? They are the remaining faithful.

They are the apple of His eye.

They are the ones He protects and provides for and cares for.

And, ultimately, they are the ones He preserves.

This is not to say that their lives are free from difficulty. When the entire garment is shredded, the remnant suffers. But the remnant has the promises and character of God to sustain it in difficult times.

This book is for the remnant: those who long to see God's name once again honored among men; those who have placed their trust in Jesus alone; those who are willing to stand against the tide of evil around them.

If you are part of the remnant, then you should know this: There's a good chance that things will get worse before they get better. And if that is the case, then everyone will suffer. Those who rebel suffer the consequences of their sin. They are walking the broad path that always leads to destruction. But I won't try to kid you. Those who are seeking to follow Christ also suffer. We suffer because we grieve over what we see. We suffer because we are swimming upstream against the current of evil. We suffer from exhaustion, loneliness, and discouragement. We suffer because sin takes its toll on our own lives; it is tough to have a good marriage and raise up godly children in these days in which we live. We suffer because every day is a battle to stay close to Christ and follow Him with our whole hearts.

I say this from experience. Last week was one of the toughest weeks Mary and I have experienced in our twenty-three years of marriage. We were hit with one devastating circumstance the first of the week, and just as we were getting our bearings by Friday, here came another. To be honest, as I write these words we are still catching our breath from the events that knocked the emotional wind out of both of us.

You've experienced weeks like that too.

But hang in there, because God is up to something. He hasn't forgotten you. He loves you. He has a plan for you *and* your children. And He will take care of you. When all is said and done, you will be able to tell of His goodness and mercy. Scripture is very clear on this point.

But if you believe judgment is coming, as I do, then there are some important questions we must ask. How can we know when a nation has reached the point of no return? What kind of judgment is God likely to send on America? If "all things work together for good to those who love God," how can good come from *this*? How in the world does a righteous man live and raise his family in times of extreme evil? If you know the answers to these questions, then the future will not take you completely by surprise. Instead, you will be prepared, with your spiritual armor intact and fitted for battle.

This is the purpose of this book. We will seek to answer these questions—first, through the study of some little-known but remarkable history, and second, through the eyes of two ancient persons of faith. One is a prophet, the other a teenager and future prophet. These two individuals lived during the same difficult time of national judgment.

The prophet is Habakkuk. His message is so fresh, it could have been written to us today. Habakkuk lived in days remarkably like those in which we live. Yet in his book we will watch him journey:

- from anxiety to acceptance,

- from worry to worship,

- from bewilderment to boldness,

- from fear to faith,

- from confusion to confidence.

How did that happen? Habakkuk came to grips with the goodness and wisdom of God, even in the midst of judgment.

The teenager is Daniel, a young man torn from his home and family at the prime of life. Daniel found himself living right in the middle of God's final judgment on Judah. We all know him for the night he spent in a lion's den. But have you ever actually looked in depth at Daniel's life? Daniel gives us an astonishingly wise and stellar example of how to live through difficult times.

The times of Habakkuk and Daniel were days of exceptional evil. Just like ours.

And very similar to the days of Noah.

Over three millennia ago, Noah and his family found themselves living in days of exceptional evil. The Bible says that "the LORD saw that the wickedness of man was great on the earth, and that every intent of the thoughts of his heart was only evil continually" (Gen. 6:5). It was so evil that "the LORD was sorry that He had made man on the earth, and He was grieved in His heart" (Gen. 6:6).

For a righteous man it was a tough time to be alive. But Genesis 6 tells us that Noah was "a righteous man, blameless in his time," a man who "walked with God." And because he did, "Noah found favor in the eyes of the LORD" (Gen. 6:8–9).

No doubt there were others who feigned belief in God. But Noah was different. Noah acted on his beliefs. And because he did, he stood completely alone. You and I may sometimes feel that we are all alone in our faith. But Noah was really alone. God said to

Noah, "*You alone* I have seen to be righteous before Me in this time" (Gen. 7:1, emphasis mine).

In such times, the temptation for Noah to compromise was relentless. It was tough to do the right thing. To remain true to his wife. To refuse the sexual temptation that came to him day in and day out. To be honest in his business dealings, even when it was to his own detriment. To say no to his children, when everyone else was saying yes. To speak up against the sinful activity that surrounded him. To be ostracized from everyone. To have no other person to support him when the attacks became unbearable. To believe that God would do what He said He would do, even though the human race had never before seen rain.

Noah and his family were it—the entire remaining remnant.

But "Noah did according to all that the LORD had commanded him" (Gen. 7:5). For 120 years Noah built the ark and preached an unpopular message. That's a long time to stand alone.

Then the unthinkable happened. The rains came, and the whole world was judged. Noah and his family alone survived. They survived in an ark, built out of sheer faith and obedience.

Harvard University was founded as a Christian school in 1636. That was only sixteen years after the landing of the Pilgrims. It was named for John Harvard, a highly respected Puritan clergyman who, by the way, believed in Noah. This may shock you, but in those days the professors at Harvard taught that the Flood was an actual historic event and that Noah was a real person, just as Jesus said. They had no problem believing that God could judge the world. In fact, they had no problem believing that God could judge them, as we will see later in this book.

But today, Harvard no longer believes the biblical account of Noah. Not because of any forthcoming evidence to the contrary, but because of a change in worldview. It has become unthinkable for any true intellectual today to believe in the existence of a personal God who is involved in the affairs of humankind. The flood has become the plot of a well-written novel, and Noah has become the main character.

I wonder what would happen if John Harvard were to visit his namesake university today and preach about Noah?

Frankly, I don't think it would shock him at all to learn that they, along with our entire culture, have decided that Noah never existed. In fact, I think he would probably get right up in the center of campus and begin to preach: "Judgment is coming. Make haste. Get in the ark!"

It's amazing, isn't it, how good preaching never grows old.

But how do you and I get in the ark today?

We get into Jesus Christ. For us, the ark is Jesus.

Are you living "in Christ"? Does He have all of your heart, or just a section of it? Do you walk with Him, like Noah? Or would those closest to you say you only act as if you are walking with Him? Do you flee sexual temptation, as Noah did? Or, late at night when no one is watching, do you find your way to pornographic websites? Are you willing to risk your reputation, even your job, by standing firm on biblical truth as Noah did? Or do you go along quietly with a dishonest deal at work?

If you're halfway in the ark, that's not going to cut it. Noah didn't go into the ark halfway. He went in completely.

It's time to get in the ark or get out.

And that's what this book is ultimately all about.

In the time of judgment, the only place to be is in the ark.

When the atomic bomb was dropped on Hiroshima, every single home within a distance of one mile from ground zero was destroyed and nearly vaporized. Except one. Just eight blocks from ground zero, one house stood virtually untouched. Scientists came and looked in amazement for an explanation. But they couldn't find one. The reason they couldn't find an explanation is that they were looking for a physical reason as to why the house wasn't destroyed. They should have looked for a spiritual reason.

It was the only house for miles occupied by Christians.

That small little house became an ark in the midst of an atomic judgment.

The blood of Jesus was over the door of that house as much as the blood of the lamb was over the doorposts in Egypt (Ex. 12).

Whenever the blood of Christ is over a house, that house becomes an ark. A mud hut in the Philippines, a cardboard house in the slums of Central America, government housing in inner-city Chicago, or a two-story house in the suburbs—they all can be turned into arks.

The ark is Jesus.

If judgment is coming, get in the ark.

If judgment is coming, get under the blood.

There is no safety or hope outside the ark.

But for those inside the ark, hope knows no boundaries or limits.

2

HANGING WITH HABAKKUK

A historian is a prophet in reverse.

—August Wilhelm Von Schlegel

OVER THREE HUNDRED years of history have proved that John Owen and Richard Baxter were not crazy. These two men pastored churches in London during the 1600s. They were two of the most respected clergymen in all of England. But sometime around 1663, some people began to wonder if these stable and conservative men hadn't taken leave of their senses.

Why?

They both began to preach that the judgment of God was about to come down on London.

This type of message was completely out of character for these two men. Neither one of them was given to extreme pronouncements. They were both careful and thoughtful scholars. There are more than twenty volumes of their work in print today, some 350 years later.

These were not extreme, unbalanced men given to sensationalism. They were sensible, godly students of the Scriptures.

But as they looked around at what was going on in England in the early 1660s, they began to see parallels to the degradation of Israel in the Old Testament. And they realized that if God would judge Israel, then He would certainly judge London. So Owen and Baxter began to proclaim this in their pulpits.

The people in their congregations listened in disbelief. London was the financial capital of the world. The whole world took its cues from the decisions made in this city. It was the seat of earthly power. It virtually controlled the commerce of the world. The British Empire was on the verge of circling the globe. Then the sun would never set on the British Empire. This was only the beginning of its greatness, they believed.

In the midst of this prosperity, these two godly men preached that judgment was coming. And they were ridiculed and scorned for their pronouncements.

On one particular Sunday, Owen declared to his congregation:

You know that for many years, without failing, I have been warning you continually of an approaching calamitous time, and considering the sins that have been the causes of it . . . I have told you that judgment will begin with the household of God; that God seems to have hardened our heart from His fear . . . and that none knows what the power of His wrath will be. In all these things I have foretold you of perilous, distressing, calamitous times . . . These now lie at the door, and are entering upon us.[1]

The people of London laughed.

They laughed until every one of the predictions that Owen made came to pass. Owen said that disease, economic chaos, and destruction of the city would come about. And it did.

In 1665, without warning, a smallpox epidemic suddenly swept through London. Within a matter of weeks, thousands were dead. There were so many bodies to bury that the people could not dig graves fast enough. Bodies were piled high on carts throughout the city.

Proud London was brought to its knees.

But they wouldn't repent.

In the middle of the night on September 2, 1666, a crazed man set fire to a row house. Within hours, London was in flames. The city had been without rain for months, and the houses and neighborhoods went up like dry tinder. The fire burned uncontrollably for four days. By the time it was over, most of the great city had been reduced to smoldering embers.

John Owen wrote:

Ah, London, London! How long has the Lord been striving with thee by His spirit, by His word, by His messengers, by His mercies, and by lesser judgments, and yet thou hast been incorrigible, incurable, and irrevocable under all! God looked at the agues, fevers, smallpox, strange sickness, want of trade, and poverty that was coming on like an armed man upon thee, with all the lesser fires that have been kindled in the midst of thee, should have awakened thee to repentance; and yet under all, how proud, how stout, how hard, how obdurant has thou been![2]

I should point out something about John Owen. What he saw coming upon London he did not see in a vision or in a dream. He saw it in the Word of God. He could see the future by looking to the past.

You and I can know the future of America by looking into God's

Word and learning from the past. Stick with me here, and I think you will begin to see it.

The Praying Prophet

If John Owen had been alive during Judah's final days, you would have probably found him hanging out with a guy named Habakkuk. Owen and Habakkuk were kindred spirits. They both lived in days of exceptional evil. They both loved God with all their hearts. They both grieved over the evil around them. And they both were compelled to speak on God's behalf to His people.

Habakkuk is a little-known prophet who spoke six hundred years before Christ. But as the book opens, you would think he had been reading our mail. If Habakkuk were to take a look around America today, he would probably think to himself that this all looks very familiar.

None of us choose when and where we are born. But God does. And God had a plan for this little-known prophet. God wanted Habakkuk to warn Judah that judgment was at hand. The evil of God's people had reached the point of no return. Their violence was rampant. Their immorality was unchecked. They encouraged wickedness. They were redefining God's laws or ignoring them outright. And the righteous were woefully outnumbered. Political leaders lived as though they were above the law. And the justice system was completely broken down.

And so Habakkuk begins his book:

The oracle which Habakkuk the prophet saw.
How long, O LORD, will I call for help,

And Thou wilt not hear?

I cry out to Thee, "Violence!"

Yet Thou dost not save.

Why dost Thou make me see iniquity,

And cause me to look on wickedness?

Yes, destruction and violence are before me;

Strife exists and contention arises.

Therefore, the law is ignored

And justice is never upheld.

For the wicked surround the righteous;

Therefore, justice comes out perverted. (1:1–4)

Habakkuk could not understand why God would let Judah sink so low without stepping in and doing something. In verse 1, we read "the oracle of Habakkuk." This word *oracle* means "burden."

Habakkuk was deeply burdened in his spirit. The nation was decaying, and God was absent. It was as though He had gone on vacation. He was nowhere to be found. He didn't respond to the prayers of the righteous. They prayed and fasted and asked God to intervene, but there was only silence. And as God's silence continued, the wickedness got worse. Instead of turning to repentance and revival, the nation grew more evil with each passing day. God's foundations were being destroyed, and truth was no longer essential. The righteous were surrounded by the powerful forces of wickedness. They were outnumbered and outgunned. Their only hope was for God to intervene and do something.

But His silence was deafening.

And Habakkuk could not understand it.

It was as though God had looked down and seen the violence, the wickedness, the lack of justice, and just turned away. How could

God turn His back on the prayers of the righteous? How could He allow the moral decay to actually get worse?

Have you ever grieved over the rapid dismantling of all that is right and good in our nation? Does the escalating violence and filth that entertain us take your breath away? Does your stomach grow weak at the unparalleled availability of sexual perversion through the Internet to anyone, at any time of the day or night, in the privacy of our own homes? Have you found yourself fighting a losing battle against the invasion of evil into the lives of your kids? Have you prayed for God to act and act soon? If so, then you, too, are a kindred spirit with Habakkuk.

In Habakkuk's day:

- the foundations were being destroyed,

- truth was no longer essential, and

- the nation was overdue for judgment.

The same is true for us.

Strip America down to her core, and you will find yourself not very far from the Judah of Habakkuk's day.

The Foundations Are Being Destroyed

In Habakkuk's day, politics were corrupt, the religious leaders had abandoned God's Word, and professing believers had begun to look just like the world around them. Evil was applauded while godliness was mocked. It was a time of staggering corruption. You were not safe even in broad daylight. When crimes were committed, the guilty got off scot-free. We know from the other prophets of the day that divorce was rampant, sexual perversion was embraced, and the people were illiterate when it came to God's Word. No one remembered his biblical roots and foundation.

Just a few years before, Judah had enjoyed the blessing of God under King Josiah. Josiah was a king who sought the Lord with his whole heart. He led the nation in a moral and spiritual revival. But under the successive leadership of his sons the nation's spiritual foundation quickly broke down.

The most important part of any structure is the foundation. Before you ever make an offer to buy a house, you pay an inspector to crawl under the house and check the foundation. If that foundation is deficient, you are in for trouble. Big trouble.

When we lived in California, a developer built three high-rise condominiums around a lake not too far from our house. It was a beautiful development. The first tower went up and sold out within a few weeks of completion. The second tower went up and was sold out by the time of completion. The third tower went up, but remained vacant for several years. What was the problem?

Shortly before this third building was completed, it was discovered that the ratios at the concrete plant had been just slightly off. Not enough that they couldn't build on the foundation, but significant enough that they couldn't allow anyone to move into the building until the foundation was strengthened. It took hundreds of thousands of dollars and more than two years of work to bolster the foundation.

There has been no more graphic illustration of the importance of quality concrete foundations than the earthquake that hit Turkey in the summer of 1999. One day Turkey was a thriving nation. The next, it was demolished. At first it was very surprising to the authorities that on the same street certain houses collapsed while others just a few feet away stood strong. But then they recognized a pattern. The houses built according to code withstood the earthquake. The ones that had bypassed the building code collapsed immediately, and usually the problem was with the foundation.

Who could have imagined that something so simple as faulty concrete slabs could lead to so many broken lives, broken families, and a broken nation?

The foundation is critical to a building. The foundation is also critical to a nation.

History You May Not Know

Judah's foundation was poured with biblical truth.

But what about ours?

This is something you won't read in a modern history book. But it is true nevertheless.

The Pilgrims were a people committed to Jesus Christ and His Word. They took their faith very seriously. And as a result, before coming to America they felt the heavy hand of persecution. So much so that they were exiled to Holland for twelve years.

When the Pilgrims stepped off the *Mayflower* onto the soil of this new land, they literally had nothing but the clothes on their back. They had little seed, few tools, no IRAs or 401Ks. They had one another, and they had their Bibles. That was it. But that's all they needed.

They began to lay down a foundation for a new nation. As they established laws for their colony, they drew directly from the Bible. The most influential book of their lives, bar none, was the Bible.

They took the principles of God's Word and began to pour the slab of our beginnings.

I cannot emphasize enough the profound significance of this. No other nation since Israel has had such biblical beginnings. And no other nation since Israel has been more blessed by God than America. In fact, the blessing on this nation has been unparalleled in history. America has been far from perfect. Yet it has become the most powerful and prosperous nation on earth. The question is "Why?" Is it because we are so ingenious, so innately gifted, so inherently able? That's what many today would like to think.

But I would submit to you that it is because our foundation is different from that of any other nation on the face of the earth. The principles of the Bible are the reinforcing bars that buttress the concrete of our moral and spiritual foundation. This is what has made us great.

I have a question for you. How come there are no families on your street picking up and moving to Iraq? Why is it that when our baseball team plays Cuba, our guys don't defect?

Cuba has a different foundation from ours. And so does Iraq.

Why have millions of people over the last several hundred years made incalculable sacrifices to bring their families here? It's because something unique was happening in this nation. There was freedom. There was value in every human life. There was a government of the people, by the people, and for the people. There was a righteous standard, upheld by the law of the land. To sum it up, there was an opportunity to make a better life. All because the foundation was square, right, and solid.

Shortly after the Pilgrims landed, they drafted a document that you may remember. It was called the Mayflower Compact. This became the first document of government for our newly beginning nation. It became a model for others to amplify and build on. Since most of us have never actually read this document, I include it here. It is brief and to the point. In case there is any question as to its Christian roots, I have put some sections in italics:

In the name of God, amen. We whose names are under-written, the loyal subjects of our dread Sovereign Lord King James *by the Grace of God* of Great Britain, France, Ireland, Kind, Defender of the Faith, etc.

Having undertaken, *for the glory of God and advancement of the Christian faith* and honor of our King and country, a voyage to plant the first colony in the northern parts of Virginia, do by these presents solemnly and mutually *in the presence of God and one of another, covenant and combine ourselves together into a civil body politic,* for our better ordering and preservation and furtherance of the ends aforesaid, and by virtue hereof to enact, constitute and frame such just and equal laws, ordinances, acts, constitutions, and offices from time to time, as shall be thought most meet and convenient for the general good of the colony. Unto which we promise all due submission and obedience. In witness whereof we have hereunder subscribed our names at Cape Cod, the 11th of November, in the year of the reign of our Sovereign King James of England . . . Anno Domini 1620.[3]

If the ACLU had been around back then, they probably would have sued the Pilgrims over this document.

There is something here of utmost importance. The Mayflower Compact was a pact, or covenant, with one another *and with God.* Throughout this book we will come back to this. The Pilgrims didn't just allude to God. They didn't just say a token prayer at the beginning of each political session. They didn't say "God bless America," and then go out and act as if God doesn't exist. They believed the Bible. They staked their lives on its authority. And they honored the God of Scripture as their very reason for existing. This is a crucial point. It is a foundational point.

The concepts in the Mayflower Compact, derived from the Bible, made up the first pour of concrete that would establish a strong foundation for a new nation. The founding fathers came along behind the Pilgrims and built on this foundation. They buttressed it and fortified it with another document that also had its moorings deep in the Word of God. And it has served us well for several hundred years.

But in your lifetime and mine, a serious shift has occurred. It is a grievous thing to watch these foundations being destroyed. Especially when the foundations showed no crack or flaws.

Noah Webster, the famous American lexicographer and statesman, said, "In my view, the Christian religion is the most important and one of the first things in which all children, under a free government ought to be instructed . . . No truth is more evident to my mind than that the Christian religion must be the basis of any government intended to secure the rights and privileges of a free people."[4]

This is a very blatant statement. Let me correct that. *In our times* it is a blatant statement. But not in Webster's time. In his time, everyone understood the value of our biblical bedrock and foundation.

If you were born after 1960, you may find this hard to imagine. But in the 1950s our culture still believed that it was good to post the Ten Commandments in the public square. Yes, Harvard and

Yale were taking the path of the "enlightened" atheistic world. But the everyday guy on the streets still believed in absolute truth. There was such a thing as right and wrong. And there were consequences to sin. These were moral absolutes, and these had held our nation together through some very tough times. The values they wove into our national fabric kept us on solid ground.

But then came the earthquake.

Moral Relativism

Although I live in Texas, I was born and raised in California. As a result, I have experienced numerous earthquakes in my life.

I have seen houses that have crumbled, bridges that have buckled, and freeways that have collapsed on top of each other. I have seen oil derricks outside of Bakersfield pulled and twisted like saltwater taffy. You see those kinds of things when you live in California for most of your life.

But the biggest earthquake that I have ever been in was a moral earthquake. It hit while I was in college in the sixties. What caused this earthquake was not the San Andreas Fault. It was a great moral fault, known as moral relativism.

Moral relativism stands opposed to biblical Christianity. It teaches that there is no Absolute Creator; therefore, there is no absolute truth. And since there is no absolute truth, everything and anything is permissible.

If someone has ever said to you, "That may be wrong for you, but it doesn't mean that it's wrong for me," then you have met a moral relativist. Moral relativism teaches that it may be wrong for you to lie, but that doesn't mean it's wrong for me to lie.

In the sixties, professors began to teach moral relativism openly and unashamedly in our colleges and universities across the land.

The result was a great upheaval across the moral skyline of our land.

Do you know what is valued most in a culture that believes in moral relativism? The answer is *tolerance*. Tolerance for every kind of evil. Tolerance for everything and everyone—*except*, of course, those who hold to moral absolutes.

Do you know what is valued most in a culture that believes in moral absolutes? The answer is *truth*. Jesus said that the truth will set you free.

Moral relativism was a direct assault on the foundations of our nation. And as we will see in a moment, it has eliminated the importance of truth. Ultimately, *there has never been a greater threat to our freedom than moral relativism.*

Several months ago I flew from Dallas to California to speak at my daughter's college. I arrived at the hotel late and called Rachel.

"Dad," she said, "chapel begins at 9:30 A.M., so I will pick you up downstairs at 8:45."

I said good-bye and called downstairs to get a wake-up call for 8:00 A.M. Then I hit the sack.

When I awoke, I glanced over at the clock. It was flashing the same irritating "12:00" it had been flashing the night before. Then I looked at my watch: 8:30! That wake-up call had never come! I had fifteen minutes to jump in the shower, shave, and get downstairs. As I was in the shower, I thought about how unreliable these hotels have become—you can't even get a wake-up call when you need it.

I made it downstairs in time. Barely. But Rachel wasn't there. That was okay. We had plenty of time. I figured she would be there by 8:55. But she wasn't. At 9:00 she still hadn't shown up. I was starting to get a little uneasy. 9:05. No Rachel. I was starting to get bothered at this point. 9:10. We had less than twenty minutes to make it to chapel and there was no sign of her!

You have, by now, probably figured out my problem.

My watch was still on Dallas time.

But I wasn't in Dallas. I was in California.

If I had asked the man standing next to me what time he had, he would have replied, "It's 7:10."

Now if I were a true relativist, I would have answered, "It may be 7:10 to you, but that doesn't mean it's 7:10 to me."

Then, of course, he would have smiled at me politely and quickly left the lobby. Nobody in his right mind thinks that time is relative. If we did, we would have chaos.

Just as God has fixed time absolutely, so He has fixed morality absolutely. And there is no changing it.

Moral relativism teaches that you can change morality to whatever you want it to be. The problem is that no moral relativist actually *lives* like a moral relativist. Try burglarizing his house, or withholding his check, or smashing into his new car. Ultimately, everyone has his own set of absolutes.

Just as you can't change time, you can't change morality.

Both are fixed by almighty God.

Moral Relativism's Coming of Age

Where are those students who were sitting in those university classrooms during the sixties, buying moral relativism hook, line, and sinker? What I am about to say may not be popular, but it is true:

They are in the Oval Office of the White House at the time of this writing.

They are federal judges.

They are senators and congressmen.

They are governors and mayors.

They are professors and college presidents.

They are corporate executives.

They are the big guys on Wall Street.

And they are destroying the foundations of this nation before our very eyes. Just as the foundation of Judah was destroyed in Habakkuk's day.

D. Martin Lloyd-Jones, pastor of Westminster Chapel in London, was one of the greatest preachers of this century. One particular Sunday morning he looked out over the congregation and said, "We are living in days of exceptional evil." They all nodded their heads in agreement.

He made that statement back in 1959.

What kind of days would Lloyd-Jones say we are living in now?

Truth Is No Longer Essential

Once the foundations are destroyed, truth is regarded as outdated, irrelevant, and utterly unimportant. In the days of Habakkuk, truth was considered no longer essential.

"The law is ignored," said Habakkuk. What law? The law of God.

"Justice is perverted," he cried out. When there are no absolutes, there is no truth. And when there is no truth, government rules according to the whim of the day. Wrong becomes right. And society becomes lawless and perverted.

How can a federal court in a free land order the Boy Scouts of America to allow homosexuals to serve as scoutmasters? How can a judge order students not to pray at a public gathering, warning that if they do they will be thrown into jail? We have made up our own truth, our own laws. And they are upside down, senseless, in the words of Habakkuk, "perverted." Truth is no longer essential, and righteousness is punished. As in the days of Habakkuk, the wicked do indeed "surround the righteous."

Habakkuk would have felt right at home here in the land of the free and the home of the brave.

For three hundred years, truth has been essential in this nation. In fact truth has been so important to us that if someone lied under oath it was a felony. That person would go to jail and carry the mark for the rest of his or her life. It could never be erased.

But when the foundations are destroyed, truth is no longer essential.

Last year I went to traffic court with my son John. We go there often. (I tell this story with John's permission.) The room was jammed, and we waited for two hours before John's name was called. As we stood before the bench, the judge looked over his papers and said, "John, I see here that you have three tickets."

John said, "No, Your Honor, I have four."

The judge looked up at John and said, "You shouldn't have told me that."

Then I said, "No, Your Honor, he should have told you that. I'm trying not to raise a Bill Clinton."

The judge looked at me and nodded knowingly.

Now it may offend you that I have taken Bill Clinton's name in vain. Perhaps you are bothered that I would use him as a negative example. The problem is this: He *is* a negative example.

If my statement offends you I would ask: Are you trying to turn your kids into Bill Clinton? Is he the standard you are trying to reach in the character development of your children?

I think not.

I think we all are trying to do better than that. I'm trying to raise children who will not lie to their spouses, to their children, or to those under whom they will serve.

And I was reminding the judge that John *should* have told him the truth.

After several minutes of dialogue, the judge said, "John, I'm going to dismiss the fourth ticket. The third ticket you can cover by going to defensive driving. As for the other two, you will be sent to Singapore to be caned." (Actually the judge didn't say that. I was hoping he would.) Suffice it to say that, as far as it was within his power to do so and still be just, he was gracious toward John.

As we left the court building and headed for the car I said, "Well, John, that judge could have been a lot harder on you, don't you think? Were you surprised?"

"I really was, Dad. I thought he would throw the book at me for that fourth ticket."

"So did I. Why do you think he didn't?" I asked.

"Dad, I think it was because I told the truth."

"I do, too, John. You don't always get rewarded for telling the truth, but you did today. You told the truth, the whole truth, and nothing but the truth. And you weren't even under oath. Do you know how refreshing it must have been for that judge to have someone just tell the truth? John, how many lies do you think that judge hears on a daily basis? How many excuses do you think he has to put up with? I'm sure it made his day to simply have someone tell the truth. How refreshing that you didn't put your hand over the microphone and consult with your attorney, and that you didn't ask him to define the word *is*. You just told the truth."

Truth is essential. You can't have a good nation without truth. You can't have justice without truth. You can't have a good marriage without truth. You can't have a good family without truth. Truth is absolutely essential and has been in this nation for three hundred years.

But no longer.

Earlier I mentioned that well-known phrase, "the truth will set you free." But let me give you the context of that phrase. In John 8:31–32, Jesus says, "*If you abide in My word*, then you are truly disciples of Mine; and you shall know the truth, and the truth shall make you free*" (emphasis mine).

Truth is the path to freedom. But this doesn't apply to everyone's "truth." It applies only to God's truth. Just as Satan is the father of lies, God is the Father of truth. All truth is God's truth. And the Bible is revealed truth. That's why the Pilgrims and the Founding Fathers built the foundations of this nation on the Bible.

Overdue for Judgment

When the foundations are destroyed and truth is no longer essential, we find ourselves in a moral free fall without a chute. This is true of individuals. And it is true of nations.

Paul describes this free fall. In chapter 1 of Romans, he outlines the steps to the demise of a nation.

1. They know God (v. 21).

2. They do not honor God or give thanks for His blessing (v. 21).

3. They turn away from His wisdom, elevating their own futile speculations (v. 21).

4. They deify man, who is corruptible (v. 23).

5. They deify animals and nature, and serve "the creature, rather than the Creator" (vv. 23, 25).

5. Lust becomes central to their culture (vv. 24, 26).

6. Homosexuality becomes rampant. Women begin to do what is unnatural and men burn in their desire toward one another—"men with men committing indecent acts and receiving in their own persons the due penalty of their error" (vv. 26–27).

7. Then God gives them over "to a depraved mind" (v. 28). Let me explain. At this point a nation is in a moral free fall. And God judges them. How does He judge them? He removes His hand of protection and blessing. He gives them over to all the resulting insidious and destructive evils. These evils spawn greater evil, until the nation begins to implode. Paul describes those who live in such days. They are:

- full of greed,

- deceitful,

- haters of God,

- insolent,

- arrogant,

- disobedient to parents,

• inventors of evil, and

• full of anger, strife, and murder.

They revel in their depravity. They are completely taken with themselves, believing that they are indestructible. They practice things that are worthy of death, writes Paul, and give hearty approval to all who do them.

At this point a nation is living on borrowed time. The blessings they have enjoyed have been from the hand of God. But now their equity is all gone, and His hand is removed.

Where is America in this spiral of decline?

Open your eyes and you will see. Homosexuality is no longer considered a destructive perversion. Instead it is practiced and embraced. And God has now given us over to depravity. We have chosen a stable economy over moral integrity and justice. That's called greed. Our children are more disobedient than any previous generation. New inventions of evil have invaded the culture through the world of cyberspace. And insolence and arrogance reign on network TV.

It has been said that America is like a great ocean liner, thrusting through deep ocean waters at full throttle. The ocean liner is a picture of power and prosperity. The people aboard are eating and drinking and making merry. They feel secure and invincible. The future is bright. Or so they think. The vessel can weather any storm that may come. The passengers have investments and stock portfolios that others envy. But there is a problem on this great ship. The engines have stopped and the boilers are broken. So how does the great ship continue to move through the waters? It is moving out of the momentum of the past. The passengers don't know it, but they are living on borrowed time, and the momentum is about to come to a halt. In due course the party will be over. Crisis will prevail.

Last night I was having my weekly Monday night devotional with Monday night football. During the break, I flipped the channel. I'd been hearing about the show *Ally McBeal*, which had become the top show of the season. It just happened to be playing opposite the game. As I flipped over, on the screen were two women—Ally McBeal and another law partner in her firm. Except for the fact that they both looked anorexic, they were attractive, sophisticated-looking women. The partner said to Ally, "Last night I had a dream. I dreamed I was kissing another woman." She looked into Ally's eyes, implying that the woman in her dream had been Ally. Then she asked her out for the evening. Ally nervously accepted the date.

I looked at my watch. It was 7:35 P.M. Prime time. The kids of America were still up.

Let me ask you a question. What kid—any kid with a sense of curiosity—is going to turn the channel now?

I decided to check back between plays to see what the kids of America are all watching. As the show progressed, Ally revealed to another friend that she was secretly drawn to the idea of kissing this woman. A male law partner gave a graphic description of how men are turned on by women involved in sex together. Another female partner described in detail her own recurring and secretly appealing sadomasochistic dream. And everyone agreed that the idea of two women kissing was really nothing to be alarmed at after all. The night ended with the date. Ally and her law partner decided that they really prefer the male sexual organ (to quote them directly). But just for fun, for the benefit of the guys standing around and watching them, they decided to pretend to be lesbian lovers engaging together in a sexually erotic dance. As they embraced and the music swelled with erotic emotion, the men hovered over them, drooling.

Great entertainment for the kids of America, don't you think?

Lust and lesbianism. And on the other channel, Jerry Springer was doing a show on sadomasochism. Will the public object? No. Meanwhile the next generation is being set up for disaster. Were you uncomfortable reading this plot? No more than I was writing it! But this is not some late-night channel on satellite TV. This is what the kids of America are watching. So we had better get real.

What occurred at the beginning of the oppression of the Jews in Nazi Germany was also deeply disturbing and embarrassing. And so people didn't discuss it at all. They simply looked the other way. Even the church of Germany refused to bring it up. They simply didn't want to rock the boat.

The truth is that America is in a moral free fall. And we are deceived to think that our children's Sunday school or youth group will offset this kind of immoral invasion into their lives. They don't have to watch it to be profoundly affected by it.

Do you grasp the cataclysmic change that has occurred in the last forty years? Do you comprehend what it means? If you do, then you, like Habakkuk, will find yourself on your knees.

Leonard Sweet tells the story of a traveler who encountered a guru on the road and asked him, "Are you a deity?"

The guru said no.

"Are you a saint?" the traveler asked.

"No," came the reply.

"Ah, then you must be a prophet!"

"No, I'm not a prophet."

"Then what are you?" asked the frustrated traveler.

"I am awake," he said.[5]

It is time for us to wake up to the fact that our nation is due for judgment. It is more than due. It is overdue.

When the foundations are destroyed and truth is no longer essential, God will not stand by. He is patient and long-suffering. He will warn us time and again. Until we have reached the point of no return.

And then judgment will come.

Just as it came upon London.

One Sunday morning John Owen looked over his congregation and proclaimed:

I am going to show you how we ought to deport ourselves in and under the distressing calamities that are coming upon us, and may reach, it may be up to the very neck . . .

Get an ark—prepare an ark for the safety of you and your families. That ark is Jesus Christ. There is no other way, no other ark—for Isaiah the prophet, said of our Lord, "And a man (Christ) shall be as an hiding place from the wind, and covert from the tempest, as rivers of water in a dry place, as the shadows of a great rock in a weary land."

That is our ark—blessed are they that trust in Him . . . I know of no safety, no deliverance, in the trials and afflictions coming upon the earth, but in believing Christ as our only refuge.[6]

I find it interesting that in his day of impending judgment, Owen implored men and women, boys and girls, to get in the ark.

That was valuable advice in 1660.

Do you know of any object from the 1600s that is not more valuable today than it was then?

An antique dresser from the 1600s is worth far more today than it was three hundred years ago.

A first-edition book from three hundred years ago would bring a price of thousands and thousands of dollars—far exceeding its original value.

So, too, for us. The value of Owen's advice has gone up astronomically.

It has been said before.

It is worth saying again.

Get in the ark.

3

CAUSE AND EFFECT

Nature is but a name for an effect Whose cause is God.

—William Cowper

As nations cannot be rewarded or punished in the next world, they must be in this. By an inevitable chain of causes and effects, Providence punishes national sins, by national calamities.

—George Mason

IT WAS JANUARY 17, 1978. A heavy snow was falling for the second time that week. Horace Becker was sound asleep in the Sheraton Hotel. At 4:15 A.M., Horace was suddenly awakened by a loud cracking noise. This wasn't a normal noise in the middle of the night. This was loud enough to raise him out of a sound sleep. He hurriedly went to the window and looked across the street to the

Hartford Civic Center Arena. This large, modern coliseum was the pride of the city. It was in constant use for basketball, hockey, and conventions. But there was a problem. The northwest section of the massive roof was actually rising, and simultaneously the center of the roof collapsed down into the coliseum. Within seconds the windows of Becker's hotel room began to shake with such violence that he thought they might blow out.

Horace hit the floor to protect himself from flying glass. Thankfully, the windows held. A few seconds later, they calmed down enough for him to take another look. The convention center was wide open. He could see the seats, the luxury boxes, and the concession stands as the roof continued to settle all the way down to the hockey ice.[1]

The roof collapsed because it couldn't bear the weight of the snow that had accumulated on it. Two other roofs collapsed that night in Hartford, but none as dramatically as that of the Civic Center. Why did it collapse? The roof simply could not handle the weight of the snow. Physics demanded that it collapse.

It is not only roofs and buildings that collapse.

Nations collapse.

The eminent historian Arnold Toynbee, in his twelve-volume work, *Civilization*, outlined the pattern of the rise and fall of great nations. Toynbee identified more than twenty civilizations that had collapsed. Each of those twenty-plus civilizations went through five stages:

1. birth

2. rapid expansion

3. conservation of gains made

4. moral decline

5. disintegration

What those civilizations had in common was that they could no longer bear the weight of their own immorality and sin. The weight of the moral decline on the roof of that civilization demanded its disintegration.

In the time of Habakkuk, Judah's roof of civilization was about to collapse.

A Disturbing Reply

Imagine with me for a minute:

If God were to reveal in advance that He was going to use China to judge America, would that not shake you to the core of your being?

If He were to indicate that He was going to allow China to defeat America and occupy and govern our nation, would that not make you sick to your stomach?

That's what happened to Habakkuk.

And prophets are only human.

Habakkuk had cried out to the Lord:

"Oh God, how can You, the holy and just God, sit silently by while injustice and evil are destroying the land? Why don't You do something?"

Then God answered his question.

But His answer was more disturbing than the question!

God told Habakkuk that justice was coming, but not in the way that this prophet would have chosen. Judah had gone too far. They had ignored Him too many times, and their own choices had now taken them beyond the point of return. God was going to judge them once and for all.

How was He going to judge them? By sending the Chaldeans:

Look among the nations! Observe!
Be astonished! Wonder!
Because I am doing something in your days—
You would not believe if you were told.
For behold, I am raising up the Chaldeans,
That fierce and impetuous people
Who march throughout the earth
To seize dwelling places which are not theirs.
They are dreaded and feared.
Their justice and authority originate with themselves.
Their horses are swifter than leopards
And keener than wolves in the evening.
Their horsemen come galloping,
Their horsemen come from afar;
They fly like an eagle swooping down to devour.
All of them come for violence.
Their horde of faces moves forward.
They collect captives like sand.
They mock at kings,
And rulers are a laughing matter to them.
They laugh at every fortress,
And heap up rubble to capture it.
Then they will sweep through like the wind and pass on.
But they will be held guilty,
They whose strength is their god. (Hab. 1:5–11)

We cannot blame Habakkuk for his astonishment at God's answer. God was about to let Judah be wiped off the map. This was unthinkable. These were God's chosen people. From them the Messiah was to come! Yet God said that He was going to send the Chaldeans to carry them away!

This was shocking news to Habakkuk. The Chaldeans, known better to us as the Babylonians, were a treacherous and evil world power on the rise. They had just knocked off Assyria—the godless and terrifying nation that had dragged away the northern kingdom of Israel only a few years before! It was like Cassius Clay defeating Sonny Liston back in the sixties. No one thought Clay could defeat the brooding, powerful man known as "the bear." But Clay defeated him and established himself as the new heavyweight champion of the world.

That's precisely what Babylon had done to Assyria. And now God was going to use a nation more powerful than Assyria and more evil than Israel to bring about their final judgment.

The news of the Babylonian invasion was almost more than Habakkuk could handle. He was shaken to the core of his being. But that news, as shocking as it was, should not have surprised Habakkuk. Why? Because Habakkuk knew Deuteronomy 28.

So what is so significant about Deuteronomy 28?

Deuteronomy 28 is the chapter of blessings and curses. And virtually every prophet who preached judgment to Israel and Judah had it on the forefront of his mind.

Cause and Effect

Deuteronomy 28 is actually one of the most significant chapters in the entire Bible. Israel's history hung in the balance of this chapter. If you were to title Deuteronomy 28, you might call it "Cause and Effect." Every effect has a cause. Every storm has its weather front. Every house has its builder. Every choice has its consequence. Cause and effect.

God gave Israel a choice. Obey Him and receive blessing. Disobey Him and receive cursing. Deuteronomy 28 is the list of those blessings and curses. It was their choice. They could have chosen the blessings. But they chose the curses instead. The sufferings they endured as a result of their sin were totally unnecessary! Yet, when given the choice, they chose God's judgment. Just as America is currently doing!

Allow me to insert a word of caution here. This concept of blessing and curses can be wrongly understood. There is a branch of teaching called prosperity theology. I do not adhere to this teaching, although there are biblical principles of prosperity. But there is also something called persecution in the Bible. Both prosperity and persecution are indications of God's approval. We will look at this in detail in Chapter 9.

Because some teaching on prosperity is deficient, we must approach this subject very carefully. Some of us have been told that any suffering or hardship in our lives is the discipline of God. Bad things can happen to godly people who are walking with the Lord. But there is a purpose behind those sufferings that cannot be ignored. We will look at this more closely in Chapters 8 and 9. For now we are going to look at a general pattern God outlined for Israel that has tremendous implications for those of us who love the Lord and seek to walk with Him.

Before we look into Deuteronomy 28, let's get the background.

The Book Behind the Chapter

You can't appreciate the chapter until you understand the context of the book behind the chapter.

Allow me to paint the picture for you.

As the scene opens in the beginning of Deuteronomy, the chosen people of God were camped out on the plains of Moab. Nearby was the Jordan River and on the other side was the Promised Land. Their mission (should they choose to accept it) was to cross the river and go in to possess the land. Since the time of their forefather, Abraham, they had dreamed of this day. It was theirs. God had promised it to them.

But it wasn't going to be a piece of cake. Even the bravest among them were scared spitless. And I'll be truthful with you. They should have been. Forty years before, their parents were in the same spot with the same mission. And they had wimped out. "Mission impossible," they had said. At least humanly impossible. Now their kids were about to go in. The anticipation of what lay ahead was no different for them than the pre-dawn hours were for our boys before they invaded the beaches of Normandy.

For one thing, their beloved leader wasn't going in with them. Not that they didn't like Joshua. But Moses was the man. The hand of God had been on Moses. As long as Moses was around, God's power and blessing were guaranteed. But now, when they needed him most, Moses was saying good-bye.

That wasn't all. The truth was that nothing had changed in Canaan since their parents had sent in the twelve spies a generation before. There were *still* giants in the land. And, if anything, the indigenous pagan nations were more violent and perverse than ever before, and their armies were bigger and better.

So here they were.

In front of them was a mighty river.

Behind them was the harsh, arid desert.

Ahead of them was a daunting task.

But the time had come.

It was now or never.

D-Day.

God commanded Moses to gather the people together. He had something important to say to them. Something that was going to go with them for the rest of their lives.

Would you have been listening? You bet. The Commander in Chief was speaking.

Moses began:

Hear, O Israel, the statutes and the ordinances which I am speaking today in your hearing, that you may learn them and observe them carefully . . .

The LORD spoke to you face to face at the mountain from the midst of the fire, while I was standing between the LORD and you at that time, to declare to you the word of the LORD; for you were afraid because of the fire and did not go up the mountain. He said, "I am the LORD your God, who brought you out of the land of Egypt, out of the house of slavery.

"You shall have no other gods before Me.

"You shall not make for yourself an idol . . .

"You shall not take the name of the LORD your God in vain . . .

"Observe the sabbath day to keep it holy . . .

"Honor your father and your mother . . .

"You shall not murder.

"You shall not commit adultery.

"You shall not steal.

"You shall not bear false witness . . .

"You shall not covet . . ." (Deut. 5:1–21, emphasis mine)

Does this have a familiar ring? Our culture may be biblically illiterate, but most Americans still recognize the Ten Commandments. That's because the Ten Commandments have been part of our heritage from the beginning.

But because we are so familiar with them, most of us have never thought about how utterly unique the Ten Commandments are among the governing laws of the world. What makes them so unique?

- They establish absolute truth.

- They declare the existence and supreme rule of the one true and living God.

- They underscore the value of every human life, elevating the status of all men as equal before God.

- They protect marriage and family, which are central to a nation's survival.

- They insist on rest, worship, and contentment—the very things that keep a nation humble and free from greed's destructive hold.

- They require honesty and unselfishness toward others, which form the hedge of safety in all human relationships.

The extraordinary nature of these laws cannot be overstated.

God said to Israel, "What great nation is there that has a god so near to it as is the LORD our God whenever we call on Him?" (Deut. 4:7).

History has demonstrated that any nation adopting the Ten Commandments as its foundation has experienced blessing and prosperity.

The Easier Way

The early American Puritans understood this. They were passionate about the Ten Commandments. They believed that the Ten Commandments were central to Christianity and to the survival of a nation. Whenever a man came to Christ in an early Puritan church, the first thing they taught him was the Ten Commandments. In fact, they taught regularly on the Ten Commandments because they believed that obedience ensures blessing.

They also believed that obedience to the Ten Commandments **was** by far the easier path in life.

The great Puritan preacher Thomas Watson wrote:

Obedience makes us precious to God, his favourites. "If you obey my voice, ye shall be a peculiar treasure unto me above all people; you shall be my portion, my jewels, the apple of mine eye" (Exodus 24:5). "I will give kingdoms for your ransom" (Isaiah 43:3) . . .

Would we have a blessing in our estates? Let us obey God . . .

Would we have a blessing in our souls? Let us obey God . . .
You lose nothing by obeying. The obedient son has the inheritance

settled on him. Obey, and you shall have a kingdom. "It is your Father's good pleasure to give you the kingdom" (Luke 12:32).

What a sin is disobedience! It is an irrational sin . . . It is a destructive sin . . .

Consider, God's commands are not grievous: he commands nothing unreasonable. (1 John 5:3) It is easier to obey the commands of God than sin. The commands of sin are burdensome; let a man be under the power of any lust, how he tires himself! What hazards he runs, even to endangering his health and soul, that he may satisfy his lusts! What tedious journeys did Antiochus Epiphanes take in persecuting the Jews! "They weary themselves to commit iniquity", and are not God's commands more easy to obey? Chrysostom says, virtue is easier than vice; temperance is less burdensom than drunkennness. Some have gone with less pains to heaven, than others to hell.

God commands nothing but what is beneficial. "And now Israel, what does the Lord require of thee, but to fear the Lord thy God, and to keep his statutes, which I command thee this day, for thy good?" (Deuteronomy 10:12–13). To obey God is not so much our duty as our privilege; his commands carry meat in the mouth of them. He bids us repent; and why? That our sins may be blotted out. (Acts 3:19) He commands us to believe; and why? That we may be saved. (Acts 15:31) *There is love in every command: as if a king should bid one of his subjects dig in a gold mine, and then take the gold to himself.*[2]

God's commands are an easy yoke. No life is easy. But this side of heaven, on a scale of one to ten, the life of obedience is a ten.

The next time you find it so hard to do the right thing, this is worth remembering. Believe me, ultimately it's easier to do the right thing.

A New Commandment

Why was Moses bringing the Ten Commandments up now in the plains of Moab? He was *reminding* this new generation about the foundation laid down by God forty years before. We have short memories. And these people had been kids when God first gave the Ten Commandments at Kadesh-barnea. They needed to hear them again.

But this time God had a deeper message for His people. It came in the form of a new commandment, a new piece to the puzzle. God did not simply want this nation to *act* in a certain way. He wanted their *hearts*. Their whole hearts. Jesus told the Pharisees that this commandment of Deuteronomy 6 was the *essence*, or sum total, of all the commandments.

Hear, O Israel! The LORD is our God, the LORD is one! And you shall *love* the LORD your God *with all your heart and with all your soul and with all your might*. And these words, which I am commanding you today, shall be *on your heart*; and you shall teach them diligently to your sons and shall talk of them when you sit in your house and when you walk by the way and when you lie down and when you rise up. (Deut. 6:4–7, emphasis mine)

If you miss this, you miss the bedrock truth of what God was about to do.

A Covenant of the Heart

God was making a covenant, or agreement, with His people. And His agreement involved their innermost hearts. Can a nation have a heart? No. A nation is made up of individuals with hearts. God wanted a one-on-one, loving relationship with each person in the nation of Israel.

This was unprecedented. It was the difference between a master-slave, king-subject, lender-debtor relationship, and a father-son relationship. God didn't want His people to be puppets or slaves. He didn't want them to walk around with long faces all day, fulfilling their duties and obligations begrudgingly. God wanted their obedience to flow out of a warm and loving relationship with Him.

That's what you want from your children, isn't it?

That's what God wants of us. Your heart matters to Him.

Have you ever noticed how the early Puritans are depicted by modern-day moviemakers? Straitlaced, dull, obsessed with duty and obligation, and just plain miserable to be around. But these are not the Puritans of the 1600s. Read about the early Puritans and you will find a very different people. One of the characteristics that set them apart was their emphasis on the heart. The Puritans believed that faith had to be more than something in your head, it had to come from your heart. And it had to change how you live in the world. The passion they felt for the Ten Commandments flowed out of a deeper passion for God.

Listen to Watson again:

God wanted Israel to live in happiness, peace, and prosperity. Everything the world wants! But He knew that only by loving Him and following Him from their *hearts* could the people hope to enter the land, conquer it, and live in peace and prosperity.

What shall we say to those who have not a drachm of love in their hearts to God? They have their life from him, yet do not love him. He spreads their table every day, yet they do not love him. Sinners dread God as a judge, but do not love him as a father . . . It is nothing but your love that God desires. The Lord might have demanded your children to be offered in sacrifice; he might have bid you cut and lance yourselves, or lie in hell awhile; but he only desires your love, he would only have this flower. Is it a hard request, to love God? Was ever any debt easier paid than this? . . .

God does not need our love. There are angels enough in heaven to adore and love him. What is God the better for our love? It adds not the least cubit to his essential blessedness. He does not need our love, and yet he seeks it. Why does he desire us to give him our heart? (Proverbs 23:26) Not that he needs our heart, but that he may make it better.[3]

What a remarkable God! What an extraordinary covenant!

God commands us to love Him—not to make Him feel good, but for our own sakes. He is not like earthly fathers. Sometimes earthly dads can get it wrong. But not God. Everything He asks of us is for our blessing.

It is worth noticing that in the brief twenty-nine verses surrounding this passage this idea is repeated six times!

". . . that it may be well with them and with their sons forever!" (Deut. 5:29)

". . . that it may be well with you, and that you may prolong your days in the land which you shall possess." (Deut. 5:33)

". . . that your days may be prolonged." (Deut. 6:2)

". . . that it may be well with you and that you may multiply greatly." (Deut. 6:3)

". . . that it may be well with you and that you may go in and possess the good land." (Deut. 6:18)

". . . for our good always and for our survival." (Deut. 6:24)

The bottom line is this: Obedience leads to blessing.

But there is another side to all of this.

Stick with me here, because this is absolutely key. *If obedience leads to blessing, then disobedience leads to a curse.* Any nation that chooses the path of disobedience has chosen the cursed path of destruction and death.

And that's where Deuteronomy 28 comes in.

Blessings and Curses

Deuteronomy 28 is sixty-eight verses in length. The list of blessings comes in the first fourteen verses. Take a moment to look at them with me:

Now it shall be, if you will diligently obey the LORD your God, being careful to do all His commandments which I command you today, the LORD your God will set you high above all the nations of the earth.

And all these blessings shall come upon you and overtake you, if you will obey the LORD your God.

Blessed shall you be in the city, and blessed shall you be in the country.

Blessed shall be the offspring of your body and the produce of your ground and the offspring of your beasts, the increase of your herd and the young of your flock.

Blessed shall be your basket and your kneading bowl.

Blessed shall you be when you come in, and blessed shall you be when you go out. (vv. 1–6)

This is fairly all-encompassing, don't you think? But there's more. Read on:

The LORD *will cause your enemies who rise up against you to be defeated* before you; they shall come out against you one way and shall flee before you seven ways.

The LORD will *command the blessing upon you in your barns and in all that you put your hand to,* and He will *bless you in the land* which the LORD your God gives you.

The LORD will *establish you* as a holy people to Himself, as He swore to you, if you will keep the commandments of the LORD your God, and walk in His ways.

So all the peoples of the earth shall see that you are called by the name of the LORD; and they shall be afraid of you.

And the LORD will *make you abound in prosperity,* in the offspring of your body and in the offspring of your beast and in the produce of your ground, in the land which the LORD swore to your fathers to give you.

The LORD will *open for you His good storehouse*, the heavens, to give rain to your land in its season and to bless all the work of your hand; and you shall lend to many nations, but you shall not borrow.

And the LORD shall *make you the head and not the tail*, and you only shall be above, and you shall not be underneath, if you will listen to the commandments of the LORD your God, which I charge you today, to observe them carefully,

and do not turn aside from any of the words which I command you today, to the right or to the left, to go after other gods to serve them. (Deut. 28:7–14, emphasis mine)

This is what God offered to Israel.

And, with a few exceptions, Israel turned Him down.

When I read this list of blessings it reminds me of how God has blessed America. I realize that this passage is dealing with Israel. But there is no doubt that the application can be made to America.

Daniel Webster understood the offer of blessing in Deuteronomy 28: "If we abide by the principles taught in the Bible, our country will go on prospering and to prosper, but if we and our posterity neglect its instructions and authority, no man can tell how sudden a catastrophe may overwhelm us and bury us and all our glory in profound obscurity."[4]

Daniel Webster had it right.

He understood the secret of where the blessings and prosperity would come from. Both have come from God's hand. His desire is to bless us. But if we wander from His truth, judgment is inevitable.

This brings us to the curses listed in Deuteronomy 28.

A Painful Promise

When you think about "curses," you probably don't usually think of God. That's because you are thinking of the kinds of curses that fill the air around your workplace everyday. Another word for this would be "profanity." But there is a second kind of curse. And this curse is the equivalent to a promise from God.

Here's an interesting fact. The curses in chapter 28 of Deuteronomy are fifty-three verses in length, as opposed to fourteen for the blessings. They are so long that I am going to include them at the end of the book in the Appendix rather than list them here. I suggest that you flip back and read through them. But allow me to warn you—these curses are not pleasant. In fact, they are so unpleasant that many never read them. They are too upsetting. Yes, they are strong. But they are strong for a reason. God wanted to keep Israel far away from sin. So He had to make the consequences severe enough to get their attention.

The curses can be broken down into seven areas of judgment. Specifically, there are at least seven different ways that God judges a nation:

1. He will send famine (vv. 17, 48).

2. He will send drought (vv. 22–24, 48).

3. He will send blight/mildew (agricultural fungus) (vv. 18, 22, 39–40).

4. He will send locusts (vv. 38, 42).

5. He will send plagues (vv. 21–22, 27, 35, 59–61).

6. He will bring about military defeat (vv. 25–26, 49–52).

7. He will bring about complete devastation (vv. 23–26).[5]

The curses were as much a part of God's covenant as were the blessings.

Living Out the Blessing

How serious was God about His covenant with Israel? Get a load of this. When the people corporately obeyed Him, you got the book of Joshua. Such miracles had not been seen since the Exodus from Egypt:

- He dried up the Jordan River so that they could just walk across into the land.

- He knocked down the walls of Jericho.

- He gave them one remarkable military victory after another. Don't forget: The Israelites had no horses or chariots, while the armies of the enemy were in some cases as numerous as "the sand that is on the seashore, with very many horses and chariots" (Josh. 11:4). Yet Israel *soundly* defeated the enemy.

- On one occasion, He sent hornets before them, driving out the enemy.

- On another He stopped the sun from its movement in the sky for an entire day so that the battle could be won (Josh. 10:13).

- He delivered to them the giants that had so terrified them forty years before (Josh. 11:21–22).

- He gave to them land on which they had not labored, cities that they had not built, and vineyards and olive groves that they had not planted (Josh. 24:13).

It was an absolutely remarkable and unprecedented period in history.

Living Out the Curses

You would think, after such blessing, that the Israelites would have stayed close to the Lord. But it took only two generations. The grandchildren of these warriors quickly forgot the name of the Lord—leading us to the next book after Joshua.

Just consider the name of that book—the book of *Judges*. The second chapter of Judges describes what happened after Joshua and the elders with him had all died: "And there arose another generation after them who did not know the LORD, nor yet the work which He had done for Israel. Then the sons of Israel did evil in the sight of the LORD, and served the Baals" (Judg. 2:10–11).

The end of Judges summarizes it all: "In those days there was no king in Israel; everyone did what was right in his own eyes" (Judg. 21:25).

It was an utterly wicked time.

The book of Judges reads like a seedy *New York Times* best-seller: "So the anger of the LORD burned against Israel," says the writer of Judges, ". . . 'Because this nation has transgressed My covenant which I commanded their fathers.'" And so, "wherever they went, the hand of the LORD was against them for evil, as the LORD had spoken and as the LORD had sworn to them, so that they were severely distressed" (Judg. 2:20, 15).

What you need to notice is this.

It didn't take long.

Judges says, "They turned aside *quickly* from the way in which their fathers had walked" (Judg. 2:17).

The decline of a nation can happen very quickly.

But Judges is only the beginning. Throughout the rest of the Old Testament we read about Israel's persistent disobedience and decline, interrupted only by intervals of judgment and repentance. It was like a broken record. Israel would wander; God would send a prophet to warn them; Israel refused to listen; God would send a curse; Israel would repent; and then God would bless them again.

For centuries God was long-suffering and patient. But after nearly one thousand years of God being patient, the nation had declined to the point of no return. So now, in the time of Habakkuk, they were about to experience military defeat and devastation.

1. He sent famine (Amos 4:6; 1 Kings 8:37).

2. He sent drought (Amos 4:7–8; 1 Kings 8:35).

3. He sent blight/mildew (Amos 4:9; 1 Kings 8:37).

4. He sent locusts and caterpillars (Amos 4:9; 1 Kings 8:37).

5. He sent plagues (Amos 4:10; 1 Kings 8:37).

6. He allowed military defeat (Amos 4:10; 1 Kings 8:37).

7. He sent complete devastation (Amos 4:11).

These were the days in which God told Habakkuk that final judgment was coming. Just like the days of Noah. Just like Sodom and Gomorrah.

Assyria had already dragged the northern kingdom into oblivion. And now Babylon was about to descend on Jerusalem and lead the last of God's chosen people away.

It was a terrible day, but an inevitable day. God was keeping His covenant. Israel would be no more.

What does all of this have to do with you and me? It has everything to do with us. Some parts of the Bible are difficult to read. But those parts are there for our benefit.

God doesn't sugarcoat reality.

And He doesn't sugarcoat the harsh consequences of sin.

We must ask again: If God judged His own chosen people, why wouldn't He judge us?

Cause and Effect, Still in Effect

The Puritans believed that He would judge us. They took Deuteronomy 28 literally.

When they arrived on this continent, they made a covenant with God. And in the years that followed, God blessed them. His providence was evident from the moment they arrived.

Peter Marshall and David Manuel describe this first generation: "The . . . legacy of Puritan New England to this nation . . . can still be found at the core of our American way of life, [and] may be summed up in one word: *covenant . . . Covenant . . .* as the Puritans demonstrated, requires total commitment."[6]

So what happened to these early committed Puritans?

In spite of their enormous influence in America, the Puritans eventually seemed to drop out of sight. Marshall and Manuel provide a fascinating answer:

One of the greatest mysteries that we faced in our search was the question of what finally became of the Puritans. They had seemed to be prospering in every way—the hard times were behind them, there was plenty of good land and plenty to eat, spacious houses, and they were living in peace with the Indians. Spiritually, for the most part, they were deeply committed, obedient, and fulfilling the terms of the covenant. And God was blessing them beyond all measure . . . Then, like a fire slowly dying down, the spiritual light began to dim, until, by the beginning of the 1700s, what had been a blazing light of the Gospel of Christ had become only a faint glow from the smoldering embers. What had gone wrong?

The more we read, the more the question plagued us, for our research was beginning to indicate that the Covenant Way was the way in which God had intended for America to go. If that were true, then the answer to the question of why the Puritans went wrong might very well provide the answer for us today.

We found our answers mostly between the lines of a number of sad accounts of such compromises as the Half-Way Covenant . . . And we found something else; countless recorded instances of what the Puritans called Divine Providence—the extraordinary intervention of

God on behalf of His people when they are in covenant with Him . . .
But we also discovered some sobering examples of Divine Justice,
when those who had been in covenant openly scorned their commitment by word and deed. And we gained a better understanding
of the judgments of God—those major and minor calamities which
a loving Father permits in order to get the attention of His wayward
children and cause them to turn back to Him. For the Puritans saw
God's intentions, for weal or for woe, as distinctly as had their spiritual ancestors in ancient Israel.[7]

I am deeply indebted to Peter Marshall and David Manuel for
the work they have done in their books. These two men have been
led on a remarkable journey by the Holy Spirit. Their journey has
led them to research libraries that are not normally open to the
public. As a result, they have uncovered material available nowhere
else. I have drawn on their research and owe a great deal to their
contributions. I heartily recommend all of their works, especially in
regard to this topic, *The Light and the Glory.*

The Birth of Halfhearted Christianity in America

The second generation of Puritans tended to live on their parents'
commitments and blessings. They believed the Bible, but their passion was beginning to wane. By the third generation fewer and fewer
were giving their hearts and lives to the Lord. They were becoming
unconverted. Yes, they still went to church, for it was the acceptable
and social thing to do. But their hearts were far from Him.

Once grown, these unconverted children wanted their own
children to be baptized in the church (as was the custom of the

Puritans who practiced infant baptism). They wanted to go through the motions of seeking God's blessing, but without changing their lifestyles. That's when "The Halfway Covenant" was devised. The Halfway Covenant was a compromise in which unconverted parents could bring their children for baptism, but they would not be allowed to take Communion. Halfway in, halfway out. In modern-day terms we would call it the Fence-Rider Covenant.

Nowhere in Scripture is there a Halfway Covenant.

Nowhere does it say that you shall love the Lord your God with half of your heart.

But they had lost their first love. They were no longer Puritans. They had become Yankees.

You've heard of the New York Yankees. What is a Yankee? If you live in the South, you tend to think of a Yankee as a Northerner. But a Yankee is more than a Northerner. A Yankee is someone who lives in the North and is self-sufficient and independent. Yankees work hard and don't need anyone else. Where did Yankees come from? Yankees are the descendants of the Puritans. They learned hard work from their grandparents who feared God, but they grew up in prosperity, and instead of depending on God to continue their blessing they depended on themselves. The Puritans became the Yankees. "And so their grandsons helped themselves to more land and moved still further away to establish their own life on their own land. There was no bothering now to gather a church first, no laws on the books which forbade inhabitants to live more than half a mile from the meetinghouse of a settled town, as there once had been."[8]

The Yankees did not need God. Or so they thought.

As this decline in faith began, the older Puritans knew that God would not stand by. So the Puritan preachers began to proclaim that judgment was coming. Not long after, judgment did come.

"Meanwhile, those men who knew the heart of God tried to alert the countrymen of their dire peril which they were surely bringing on themselves. For God was warning them directly, with droughts, with plagues of locusts and caterpillars, with smallpox epidemics, and with all the myriad and seemingly unconnected things which start to go wrong when grace is lifted."[9]

The Puritans did not believe that caterpillars overrunning their crops and smallpox breaking out in a town were random, chance acts of life. They saw them as the disciplining hand of God judging His people when their hearts wandered from Him. Or, to put it another way, it was cause and effect.

In their minds the caterpillars were a judgment from God. There was sin in the camp. The smallpox was another indicator. These incidents were not separate, they were linked together! The preachers were quick to remind the people of what was happening. And they called the people to repentance. But just a handful took their warning seriously.

And so God, in His great love, had to follow the caterpillars with chastenings and warnings progressively more severe. Repeatedly, His people would turn back to Him, and pray and call His name and humble themselves, and He would gladly relent and return their blessings. But each time they were a little more quick to turn away again and each time their repentance was a little more perfunctory— a going through the motions, with not everyone bothering to observe the fast days or attend the services. And while there may indeed have been repentance in the hearts of many, it did not reach deeply enough to affect an amending of lives, for their hearts were turning hard and dry like Israel's of old. And so the droughts did not lift so quickly, nor did the pests entirely disappear.[10]

The judgments continued and became more intense and widespread.

By 1670 the difficulties in Massachusetts had become so great that the government undertook a special investigation to find out why God was afflicting the state with such sickness, crop failure, and losses in business.[11]

Michael Wigglesworth wrote a poem that was widely quoted across New England at the time. It is entitled "God's Controversy with New England." Here is a sampling of several verses:

Our healthful days are at an end and sicknesses come on
From year to year, because our hearts away from God are gone,
New England, where for many years you scarcely heard a cough.
And where physicians had no work, now finds them work enough.

Our fruitful seasons have been turned of late to barrenness,
Sometimes through great and parching drought, sometimes through rain's excess,
Yea now the pastures and cornfield for want of rain do languish;
The cattle mourn and hearts of men are filled with fear and anguish.

The clouds are often gathered as if we should have rain;
But for our great unworthiness are scattered again.
We pray and fast, and make fair shows, as if we meant to turn;
But whilst we turn not, God goes on our fields and fruits to burn.[12]

It was all coming their way. Grasshoppers were eating their crops, drought was scorching their land, floods were bringing ruin and destruction, and sickness was wiping out families. These were all warnings. But it didn't seem to get their attention. What *would* it take to get their attention? It would take war, torture, and mutilations.

A More Severe Judgment

After the Puritans had lived in peace with the Indians for years and seen many of them converted, a handful of Indians who hated Christianity began a series of shocking raids. These raids were lead by a Chief Philip of the Wampanoags. Philip and medicine men who hated Christianity declared war on the settlers. On June 21 they attacked the small settlement of Swansea, just outside of Plymouth Colony. They murdered, mutilated, and burned the inhabitants—men, women, and children. "When the colonial troops finally arrived, they were shocked and sickened at the horror of the scene which confronted them. The main street of the little village was strewn with the dismembered corpses of men, women, and children. So hideous was the sight that it did not even register at first that it could have been done by human beings. Satan had unleashed his fury on New England."[13]

Philip had an army of fifteen hundred braves, larger than that of the colonists. He continued to raid and kill.

New England was totally unprepared, strategically, mentally and spiritually. A company of militia would be hastily called out and dispatched to the relief of a beleagured town or hamlet, only to be cut to pieces by a well-placed ambush waiting for it. A second column would be sent to the aid of the first, only to blunder into a separate ambush set for it. And so it went, until the settlers were afraid to go into the woods, let alone vigorously pursue the enemy. Throughout

New England, morale had sunk to its nadir, for into the towns not yet under attack came the survivors—some in hysterics, others dumbstruck by atrocities beyond the human mind's capacity to assimilate. Almost immediately, a fast day was declared in Massachusetts, but no sooner had the service ended, than reports of fresh disasters arrived. Clearly this time God's wrath was not going to be turned aside by one day's worth of repentance.[14]

The preachers of New England continued to tell the people that these attacks had not happened by chance. The hand of God was in this. By this time every Indian tribe in New England had joined in the attacks, and there wasn't a safe place to be found. Two of the most well-known preachers, father and son, Increase and Cotton Mather, preached from Jeremiah:

Behold, I am bringing upon you . . . a nation whose language you do not know . . . Their quiver is like an open tomb, they are all mighty men. They shall eat up your harvest and your food; they shall eat up your sons and your daughters . . . they shall eat up your vines and your fig trees; your fortified cities in which you trust they shall destroy with the sword.

They lay hold on bow and spear, they are cruel and have no mercy, the sound of them is like the roaring sea; they . . . set in array as a man for battle, against you, O daughter of Zion! (Jer. 5:15–17; 6:23 RSV)

Finally the people began to listen.

The Bay Colony's churches filled, and people who had not attended church in years stood in the aisles and joined in prayers. For the battle was a spiritual one; and even the most pragmatic among them were coming to see that. God's patience with the colonists' hypocritical ways had come to an end. He was not about to relent and restore the saving grace, which had so long protected them and which they had so long taken for granted, unless the whole fledging nation had a change of heart.[15]

If you were to have asked the average colonist what was occurring, he would have told you that the judgment of God was upon them. They knew it, and the government officials knew it. They had wandered far from Him, and after they refused to heed His disciplinary measures, He sent crushing military defeat. Cause and effect.

The Righteous Remnant

You may be asking, "But what about those who remained faithful through it all? What about the remnant?"

I'm glad you asked. Because a close examination of what happened shows the goodness, mercy, and blessing of God upon those who followed Him with their whole hearts:

Many of those families and settlements which were now being hardest hit had long removed themselves far from the churches, physically as well as spiritually. Moreover, many of these families had incorporated into towns without first gathering a church. And the Mathers were making it abundantly clear that their misfortune was no coincidence . . .

But where even the most isolated settlements had striven to keep faith with God and with one another, God kept faith with them.

According to a history of the town of Sudbury, the reason that Sudbury rather than Concord was chosen by the Indians as their next point of attack was that the Indians feared the influence that Concord's minister, Edward Bulkey, had with the Great Spirit. The history quotes an old Indian chronicle as follows: "We no prosper if we burn Concord," they say. "The Great Spirit love that people. He tell us not to go there. They have a great man there. He great pray."[16]

Why did the Indians pass over Concord?

Edward Bulkey had gotten in the ark.

And that godly leader's life was honored by the Lord.

There are numerous stories of faithful families and townships that came under attack, but God would divert the militia another way, and they would be rescued just in the nick of time. Episodes like this happened time and time again. "Even in New England's darkest hour, God's judgment could be seen to be tempered with mercy on behalf of his faithful."[17]

God knows who His people are. He knows those who are following Him with their whole hearts. And so, while the majority of New England were living under the curses of Deuteronomy 28, the remnant were still blessed by God.

Repentance and Grace

Finally the colonists began to listen to the Lord in earnest:

Not in twenty years had Increase Mather preached so often to such capacity crowds. And for the first time in even longer than that, people were listening to every word—and not just hearing but heeding. In the face of the repeated successes of the Indians, the much-vaunted Yankee self-reliance and self-confidence melted away like a candle on a hot stove. A great many farmers and backwoodsmen knew the taste of fear for the first time in their lives, and got down on their knees, some also for the first time. By April of 1676, there was scarcely a man or woman in all of New England who was not diligently searching his or her own soul for unconfessed sin or unrepented sin. In fact, it became unpatriotic not to do so—as if one were not doing one's part for the war effort.[18]

When the people repented, something happened. The advantage in the war began to turn. And who did God use to turn the advantage to the now-praying colonists? He used Indians to give them the advantage. Christian Indians who loved the Lord with all of their hearts. Many colonists believed that the only good Indian was a dead Indian. But many of these Indians were strong believers in Jesus Christ, and condemned Chief Philip and the medicine men who were committing the atrocities.

Many of these believing Indians, known as "Praying Indians," were at first under tremendous suspicion and harsh treatment by the colonists. But a number of preachers stepped in to protect these new brothers and sisters in Christ. Many of these "Praying Indians" were held captive on an island in Boston Harbor. In the midst of very trying conditions, their character and attitudes began to show that they could be trusted. They were then given arms and the responsibility of scouting for the colonists. Then they began to instruct the colonists in Indian tactics—how to counter them and even use them for their advantage.

It was the wisdom and counsel of these "Praying Indians" that turned the tide of the war in the colonists' favor. Chief Philip (or

King Philip, as he preferred to be called) was ambushed one night when a deserting Indian came to the colonists and offered to lead them to Philip. That, essentially, brought the war to an end.

The Indian War exacted from New England a heavy, heavy price. "The aftermath of the war which cost proportionately more lives than any other war in America's history, and loaded the survivors with crippling debt, nonetheless proved salutary. Prosperity was indeed lost, but God's New Israel was saved—for a season."[19]

For a season. Until the cycle would begin all over again.

A New Way of Seeing

Considering what you have just read, do you now understand the events around you a little more deeply? Do you recognize the hand of God? Do you understand that cause and effect are still in operation today?

Our early fathers believed strongly in the blessings and curses. They believed that if they followed after the Lord with their whole hearts, He would give them protection and peace. He would bless their businesses, their harvest, and their physical health. But they also believed that if they disobeyed, they would begin to see His judgment.

In our hearts and spirits we sense that judgment is coming. This moral free fall cannot continue without God responding. And respond He will.

The Puritans saw this happen.

Habakkuk saw it happen.

Tell me, why would we not see it happen?

4

PROSPERITY:
THE LAST CHAPTER BEFORE
JUDGMENT

Religion begat prosperity and the daughter devoured the mother.

—Cotton Mather

IF HABAKKUK WERE to visit America, one distinguishing mark would immediately catch his attention—our unprecedented prosperity.

It wouldn't be his first exposure to prosperity.

Judah was enjoying phenomenal prosperity when Habakkuk was alive. Certainly there was corruption, injustice, violence, and unchecked immorality. But there was also a booming prosperity that couldn't be stopped.

Or so they thought.

Then God sent judgment and the prosperity came to a crashing halt.

There is one point that will be our focus for the next two chapters. *The last thing a merciful God does before He sends all-out, unrestrained, and unbridled judgment on a nation is to send them all-out, unrestrained, and unbridled prosperity.*

Did you get that? For most of us, this is an unexpected cause and effect. Yet, as we are about to discover from the pages of Scripture, prosperity is actually part of the curse of God upon an evil, rebellious nation.

I know what you are probably thinking. Prosperity? A curse? No way. Sure, prosperity makes us complacent. And maybe a little selfish. But isn't a booming prosperity the sign of plain old healthy, all-American capitalism at its best? Isn't it the reward for hard work and industrialism? How could prosperity possibly be that bad?

It can't be. Unless you know the Scriptures.

If you know the Scriptures, God will give you insight into what is about to happen and what you can do to prepare. That's why these next few chapters are so critical for you and your family.

It was David Wilkerson who first got me thinking about this from a biblical perspective. In his book *America's Last Call*, Wilkerson points out that prosperity is always the last stage before judgment.

Think about it.

What preceded the judgment of the Flood?

Prosperity.

What preceded the judgment on Sodom and Gomorrah?

Prosperity.

What preceded the final judgment on Israel that Amos prophesied?

Prosperity.

What preceded the judgment on Judah when it was taken into captivity in Babylon?

Prosperity.

What preceded the seven years of judgment on the Babylonian king Nebuchadnezzar?

Prosperity.

Are you starting to notice a trend?

Go beyond the history of the Old Testament, and the pattern continues.

Prosperity preceded the fall of the Greek and Roman civilizations, as it has preceded the fall of civilizations throughout history.

At the height of Greek culture, greed ruled the land. In his excellent study of the history of civilizations, Carl Wilson writes in his book *Man Is Not Enough* that at the height of Greek culture, there was such "a feverish struggle for money" that the Greeks actually invented a new word, *pleonexia,* to describe the appetite for "more and more," and another new word, *chremastisticke,* to describe the frantic pursuit of riches. Wilson writes: "Goods, services, and persons were increasingly judged in terms of money and property. Fortunes were made and unmade with a new rapidity, and were spent in lavish displays that would have shocked the Athens of Pericles."[1]

And get this little side note. Historical sources show that simultaneously, lawsuits over money among the Greeks began to proliferate. Lawsuits? Over money? What kind of insanity is this?

Rome was no different. I will not take the time to enumerate the vast evidence available to us regarding the unbridled pursuit of pleasure and wealth before Rome's final collapse. Rome's prosperity was such that Edward Gibbon, well-known Roman historian, tells us that the government basically fed the poor masses. The dependence on this governmental handout was so great that Gibbon lists this support of the poor as one of the five top reasons for the downfall of Rome. Can you imagine it? An entire subgroup of people who, rather than working for their food, depended on the government to put bread on their table?

But of course you can. Hence, we know from history that America is in trouble.

Suffice it to say that it was Rome that was clearly on the mind of the apostle Paul as he wrote the first chapter of Romans.

Think back again to that chapter. The final stage in a nation's decline, said Paul, was the point at which "God gave them over to a depraved mind" (1:28). But what is it that happens when God gives them over? Follow this closely. Paul brings up murder, strife, deceit, inventors of evil, and the like (1:29–30). But before all of these, he speaks of another *more basic and destructive evil*. That evil is "greed" (1:29). Why greed? I would suggest to you that it is because greed leads to the unrestrained pursuit of wealth and prosperity. And the unrestrained pursuit of wealth and prosperity always leads to a host of manifold and destructive evils.

Lest there be any question as to the truth of this, look at another passage of Scripture. Paul is advising his young disciple Timothy in the disciplines of Christian faith. And, as is Paul's custom, he cuts right to the chase: *"The love of money is the root of all evils"* (1 Tim. 6:10 RSV, emphasis mine).

Did you catch that? *All* evils. The Bible is clear.

Now I have a question for you. If the love of money really is the root of all evils, then what does this mean for you and me? And on a bigger scale, what does it mean for America?

Two Kinds of Prosperity

All prosperity comes from God.

There are actually two kinds of prosperity God brings to a nation.

The first is a prosperity that comes as a blessing from God. When individuals or nations walk in obedience to the Lord, obeying His commands and statutes, God blesses them. This kind of blessing usually comes early in the life of a nation that follows the Lord. When they walk in obedience, they receive the kind of blessing and prosperity that He promised in Deuteronomy 28. And this prosperity honors God and lifts His name high among the nations of the world.

This is the kind of blessing that God gave to America from its very beginning.

The second kind of prosperity comes as a curse from God. This is the prosperity of the wicked, and usually comes later in the life of an individual or nation. The nation begins to break down morally and spiritually. There is no concern for God. God's laws are ignored, mocked, and ridiculed. In due time, the pursuit of money becomes god. And greed becomes the religion of the masses. In this prosperity, God allows mankind to experience the sad consequences of his own sinful ways.

This is the prosperity that always comes before sudden and terrible judgment.

Go with me back to the days of Noah.

Noah and Prosperity

Jesus referred to the days of Noah in Luke 17 when He was teaching the disciples about His second coming. Let's begin with verses 26–27 of Luke, chapter 17, with the words of our Lord: "And just as it happened in the days of Noah, so it shall be also in the days of the Son of Man: they were eating, they were drinking, they were marrying, they were being given in marriage, until the day that

Noah entered the ark, and the flood came and destroyed them all."

Do these verses describe a time of prosperity? People eat and drink and get married when times are good and when times are bad. So how do we know that the days just prior to the Flood were actually days of prosperity? Let's go back to Luke 17 and read the rest of Jesus' comments: "*It was the same as happened in the days of Lot:* they were eating, they were drinking, they were buying, they were selling, they were planting, they were building; but on the day that Lot went out from Sodom it rained fire and brimstone from heaven and destroyed them all" (Luke 17:28–29, emphasis mine).

Jesus is describing the days of Lot, equating them to the days of Noah. But here, as He describes the conditions before the judgment on Sodom, He gives us a little more insight. He now says that there were buying and selling. Of course, people do that in bad economic times too. They just don't do a lot of it.

But read on. Jesus indicates that there was an extraordinary amount of buying and selling. In fact, He says they were *building*. And that's the tip-off.

Any economist will tell you that one of the signs of prosperity is building. I remember flying into Dallas in the early eighties. As I rode downtown with the gentleman who picked me up, he said in half jest, "Welcome to Texas, where the state bird is the crane." He didn't mean the whooping crane. He meant a construction crane. As we approached downtown, I looked out over the horizon and counted somewhere in the neighborhood of fifteen massive cranes spread out across the city. Those cranes were the sign that an economic boom was in process. The early eighties were tremendous times of prosperity in Texas. Anybody who was around then will tell you this—people were making money hand over fist.

I remember meeting on this trip a college student who was wearing a ten-thousand-dollar solid gold Rolex on his wrist. The building boom was so strong that this college student was running a construction company part-time. He was cleaning up, working just twenty-five hours a week. Yep. Money was flowing in Texas, and it wasn't just from oil.

Building is always a sign of prosperity. And vice versa. When the economy goes south, so do the cranes. When the boom went bust in Texas a few years later, there wasn't a crane to be seen for miles. They were gone. And they left so suddenly that it was not unusual to see half-finished high-rise office buildings sitting vacant, with absolutely no activity around them.

When prosperity is in full force, people build like crazy.

But when the economy is in bad shape people don't build. Because, of course, there's no money to build.

That's why you will often hear on the financial news networks a report on "housing starts." What is the big deal about "housing starts"? It's very simple. The amount of new homes that are under construction is one of the signs that economists look at to determine the condition of the economy. When "housing starts" are up, it's an indication of prosperity. People have got the money to move up to a bigger house.

Likewise, when "housing starts" are way down, the economy is hurting.

So when Jesus tells us that in the days of Noah and Lot they were "building," He's letting us know that there was significant prosperity. They were eating steak instead of hamburger. They were drinking vintage wines instead of the cheap stuff. They were marrying and giving away in marriage, and they were having the receptions at the country club . . . with a catered sit-down dinner! That's prosperity!

But notice something else.

They had it, right up until the moment the Flood came.

And they had it, right up until the moment that God sent destruction on Sodom and Gomorrah.

If there's any doubt as to the prosperity of Sodom and Gomorrah, Ezekiel settles the question: "Behold, this was the guilt of your sister Sodom: she and her daughters had arrogance, *abundant food*, and *careless ease*, but she did not help the poor and needy. Thus they were haughty and committed abominations before Me. Therefore I removed them when I saw it" (Ezek. 16:49–50, emphasis mine).

Abundant food and careless ease! They didn't just have food, they had abundant food. They had whatever they wanted. They were building the finest homes, and they were eating the finest food. And they enjoyed "careless ease." They had so much prosperity that they didn't have a care in the world. That's what the word *careless* means. It literally means "to be without care." The wealthy Sodomites were lounging around looking for something to interest them! Were they idle because there was no work? No! They were idle because they didn't have to work! They were prosperous!

That's the kind of prosperity there was in Sodom, right up until the day of judgment.

In the days of Noah, prosperity was the chapter before judgment.

In the days of Sodom and Gomorrah, prosperity was the chapter before judgment.

Prosperity and the Habakkuk Connection

Habakkuk lived under the reign of Josiah and his three sons.

Are you familiar with King Josiah? He was the greatest king of Judah. Greater than King David or even his son Solomon. I did not say this, the Bible says this, as we will see in a moment. Josiah was a godly man, through and through. God blessed him abundantly. Josiah came on the scene in a day of unprecedented evil in the life of Judah. Yet the power of his godly leadership completely turned around the spiritual condition of Judah . . . for a time.

Before Josiah's ascension to the throne, God was ready to destroy Judah. The evil in the land had reached an all-time low. Josiah's grandfather Manasseh had been the most wicked king in Israel's history. And Amon, Manasseh's son, was so wicked that a short time into his reign his own servants assassinated him. So, due literally to the immorality of his own dad, little Josiah took the throne at the age of eight. It was a grim and pivotal moment in the life of the nation of Judah.

But God did a most remarkable thing in the heart of this young boy-king. God converted his heart. It was an act of grace for Josiah and for Judah. And so, at the age of sixteen, Josiah "began to seek the God of his father David; and in the twelfth year he began to purge Judah and Jerusalem" (2 Chron. 34:3). Josiah tore down every idol, grinding them to ashes, and cleared the land of every priest, every sacrament, every shred of evidence of wicked idol worship. The entire kingdom was purged. Josiah was just twenty when he did these things.

Then Josiah ordered the rebuilding of the temple. The temple was in shambles from the judgment and shame of the previous century.

In the midst of clearing the rubble, a priest discovered the book of the law of God, given by Moses. It had been there for decades, gathering dust and cobwebs and who knows what else. The ink was probably faded from exposure to the elements over time. But when he discovered it, the priest brought this ancient treasure to Josiah. "Read it to me!" commanded Josiah.

You've got to realize that this was the first time Josiah had ever heard the Scriptures. The very first time. As Josiah heard the words of the law, he was deeply moved. The Bible tells us that "when the king heard the words of the law . . . he tore his clothes" (2 Chron. 34:19). Josiah was grieving over the sins of the nation. He called for a godly prophetess named Huldah to help him understand the words he was hearing. And guess which part of Scripture he asked her to explain? It was Deuteronomy 28 (2 Chron. 34:24–25). A remarkable coincidence? Nothing is coincidence when God is at work.

Josiah read the blessings and curses of Deuteronomy 28. Immediately he realized the implications for the nation. Under his father and grandfather, certain curses had already come down upon the people. The people and their land had suffered greatly. But now Josiah's tender heart could see the enormity of their great sin. Josiah realized that if God were true to His promise, judgment was inevitable.

Huldah prophesied that Josiah was right. The day of God's great wrath was indeed very near at hand. But, she conveyed, "'because your heart was tender and you humbled yourself before God, when you heard His words against this place and against its inhabitants, and because you humbled yourself before Me, tore your clothes, and wept before Me, I truly have heard you,' declares the LORD" (2 Chron. 34:27).

God promised Josiah that He would withhold judgment during his lifetime. And God did just that.

What happened next demonstrates Josiah's sincere and repentant heart for his people. He gathered the people together, read the law to them, and as their king, made a public covenant with God "to keep His commandments and His testimonies and His statutes *with all his heart and with all his soul*" (2 Chron. 34:31, emphasis mine.)

Deuteronomy became Josiah's book to live by. As a result, the rest of Josiah's reign was a time of tremendous blessing. One of the first projects Josiah undertook was the rebuilding and restoration of the temple. He did this when he was twenty-six years old. Notice this: King Josiah was building. And building means prosperity.

It would appear that under the reign of Josiah there was a revival in the land. The people put away their idols. They worshiped God once again.

And so, for a season, God prospered the land and stayed His hand of judgment upon Judah.

A One-of-a-Kind Guy

Josiah was truly one of a kind. No king outdid him in pursuing God. Here is the eulogy declared upon his death: "And before him there was no king like him *who turned to the LORD with all his heart and with all his soul and with all his might, according to all the law of Moses; nor did any like him arise after him*" (2 Kings 23:25, emphasis mine).

What a tribute to a man who simply loved God with all his heart! We could use some little Josiahs running around today, couldn't we? There is no question that Josiah's life impacted an entire nation at a very crucial time.

But there is also a sad part to this story. Josiah was a bright light in a very dark world. As soon as Josiah died, so did the light. The revival was over. Everybody had been riding on the coattails of this man. Josiah had repented, and a small minority with him. But the repentance of the nation had been superficial at best.

May I ask you a probing question? Are we seeing the same thing today? In my part of the country, there are churches that hold something they call a "revival." They actually put them on our calendars.

They schedule them to occur in a particular church on a particular night of a particular week of a particular month of the year. They bring in a speaker, and they all come together. They sing. They pray. Sometimes they cry. They promise to live a godly life. And then everyone goes home. But is this really revival?

You see, when true revival sweeps through a church, or a town, or a nation, something extraordinary happens.

Listen to what Martin Lloyd-Jones had to say about revival:

What is meant by a revival? It is an experience in the life of the church when the Holy Spirit does an unusual work. He does that work primarily amongst the members of the church; it is a reviving of the believers. You cannot revive something that has never had life.

So revival, by definition, is first of all an enlivening and quickening and awakening of lethargic, sleeping, almost moribund church members. Suddenly the power of the Spirit comes upon them and they are brought into a new and more profound awareness of the truth they had previously held intellectually, and perhaps at a deeper level too. They are humbled, they are convicted of sin, they are terrified at themselves. Many of them feel that they have never been Christians. And then they come to see the great salvation of God in all its glory, and to feel its power.

Then, as a result of their quickening and enlivening, they begin to pray. New power comes into the preaching of the ministers, and the result of this is that large numbers who were previously outside of the church are converted and brought in. So the two main characteristics of revival are, first, this extraordinary enlivening of the members of the church, and, second, the conversion of masses of people who hitherto have been outside in indifference and in sin.[2]

If Lloyd-Jones is right, and I think that he is, we have yet to witness a true national revival in your lifetime or mine. Does this mean that individuals have not been revived? Absolutely not. Just as with Josiah, personal revivals do occur. Countless thousands of men have been transformed at Promise Keepers meetings. And God is working in other ways in our times. I meet men and women everywhere I go whose lives have been radically changed by the Spirit of God. And for this we are grateful to God.

But listen carefully.

It is entirely possible to be caught up in the thrill of an event: the excitement of being together in a stadium full of men, or the emotion of a message or concert. It is possible to move with the crowd, do as the crowd, pray with the crowd, make promises with the crowd, even *speak before* the crowd, and yet *never ever really do serious business with God in your own heart.*

That happens.

It happens a lot.

It happens in our day, and it happened in Josiah's day.

It is human nature.

Especially when you are living in days of prosperity.

That's exactly what happened in Josiah's day.

Underneath the impressive veneer of the newly "revived" nation was a dark, hidden life, waiting for the day that the light would go out. The majority of Judah still had a hard heart toward God.

The prophet Jeremiah prophesied in the days of Josiah. And he saw through their hypocrisy. Note the diagnosis of their hearts that this spiritual cardiologist declares:

The word that came to Jeremiah concerning all the people of Judah . . . "From the thirteenth year of Josiah the son of Amon, king of Judah, even to this day, these twenty-three years the word of the LORD has come to me, and I have spoken to you again and again, but you have not listened. And the LORD has sent to you all His servants the prophets again and again, but you have not listened nor inclined your ear to hear . . . 'Because you have not obeyed My words, behold, I will send and take all the families of the north,' declares the LORD, 'and I will send to Nebuchadnezzar king of Babylon, My servant, and will bring them against this land, and against its inhabitants, and against all these nations round about; and I will utterly destroy them, and make them a horror, and a hissing, and an everlasting desolation.

'Moreover, I will take from them the voice of joy and the voice of gladness, the voice of the bridegroom and the voice of the bride, *the sound of the millstones [business, commerce, and prosperity], and the light of the lamp.*

'And this whole land shall be a desolation and a horror, and these nations shall serve the king of Babylon seventy years.'" (Jer. 25:1, 3–4, 8–11, emphasis mine)

Here it is again. They had prosperity that came from the Lord. But that prosperity didn't soften their hearts; rather, it hardened their hearts. It gave them a false sense of security.

In a sense, *feigned repentance is worse than no repentance at all.*

Jesus painted a vivid picture to illustrate this truth:

He who is not with Me is against Me; and he who does not gather with Me, scatters.

When the unclean spirit goes out of a man, it passes through water-less places seeking rest, and not finding any, it says, "I will return to my house from which I came." And when it comes, it finds it swept and put in order. Then it goes and takes along seven other spirits more evil than itself, and they go in and live there; and the last state of that man becomes worse than the first. (Luke 11:23–26)

Jesus is describing a man who has essentially said, "I will clean up my heart. I will get rid of the pornography. I will put away my hunger for money and success. I will follow a right path. I promise." So this man cleans up his act for a while. But his heart is empty. He doesn't really know God. He doesn't really walk with God. He doesn't make the tough long-term choices—and, make no bones about it, they are sometimes very tough choices—that a man who loves Christ will have to make in his life. What happens to this man? The empty heart is still empty when the unclean spirit returns.

I tell you with a grieving heart that this is very serious stuff. My heart is grieving over this because someone very close to me is in this exact position as I write these words. And those of us who love this person are warning him, but he doesn't see the danger. This person thinks he can handle it on his own. But that is the pride of the flesh. What is needed in this person's life is a broken spirit that cries out to God for mercy and grace.

Anything less is a synthetic repentance. It is a false repentance. That's why it doesn't stand the test of time. It is not from the heart. It is a repentance only of the mouth. And it is empty.

A man who does such a thing is asking for God's judgment. God is not fooled by a smooth and winsome exterior.

Likewise, a nation that goes to church and carries the Bible and puts "In God We Trust" on its money and prays before congressional sessions—yet simultaneously tramples His truth, mocks His name, aborts His children, glorifies perversion, and spits on the blood of His Son, is a nation headed for swift and severe judgment.

Such was the case in the days following Josiah's death.

To Jehoiakim, Josiah's son who succeeded him to the throne, Jeremiah prophesied: "I spoke to you in your prosperity; but you said, 'I will not listen!'" (Jer. 22:21).

A child born into prosperity often does not appreciate the price that has been paid for that prosperity. Unless his heart is converted, he will enjoy the prosperity free of charge, like a credit card. He will use it for his own desires, mounting up a debt of unthankfulness and pride. And prosperity and pride are a lethal combination.

Habakkuk lived during the revival of Josiah. And he was there when the moral decay spread like gangrene under Josiah's son Jehoiakim. It was the corruption and violence of Judah under Jehoiakim that caused Habakkuk to cry out to God (Hab. 1:1–4). But the prosperity of Jehoiakim was going to end swiftly. Judgment would no longer be stayed. The prosperity of Jehoiakim was the last stage before God sent judgment.

Prosperity comes before judgment. It happened in Noah's day. It happened in Lot's day. It happened in Habakkuk's day. And it is happening in our day.

Wilkerson sets it out plainly:

Throughout the Scriptures, we detect a pattern. Whenever nations turned away from God, he sent them warning through prophets. If the people didn't respond, God often sent them violent storms and drastic weather changes and plagues to wake them up. And if that didn't work, God sent them one final message: he inundated them with prosperity. It was a last, great mercy call!

In most cases, the people despised God's blessings and goodness, turning to indulgence. And when that happened, judgment quickly followed. Paul writes: ". . . Or do you think lightly of the riches of His kindness and forbearance and patience, not knowing that the kindness of God leads you to repentance? But because of your stubbornness and unrepentant heart you are storing up wrath for yourself in the day of wrath and revelation of the righteous judgment of God, who will render to every man according to his deeds" (Rom. 2:4–6).

God is saying, "My day of reckoning is coming upon you. And you know you deserve my wrath and judgment! Yet, by sending you all these present blessings, I mean to woo you to repentance. My goodness to you is meant to reveal your unworthiness and to humble you. But if you continue to despise my blessings and walk in blatant sin, you'll only store up my wrath against you!

Day after day, our prosperity here in America grows. Yet we have not humbled ourselves. We're storing up God's wrath against us—and soon he'll pour it out."[3]

Wilkerson is exactly right. And in godly hearts, that message rings true.

The World's View on Prosperity

If you don't think biblically about prosperity, it can get you into trouble. The thing about prosperity is that it lulls you into thinking that you aren't in trouble. Benjamin Franklin warned, "Abundance, like want, ruins men."

Prosperity is infectious.

Prosperity lulls us into moral and spiritual stupification.

Prosperity says you can make it on your own.

Prosperity says life will always be this way.

Prosperity says that you are the one responsible for your wealth.

Prosperity says that you are secure.

Prosperity says that you are financially set for the future, no matter what comes.

Prosperity says that what you have is good, but more would be better.

Prosperity says that you have what it takes to get through any problem.

Prosperity says that you don't need God.

You *are* a god.

That's literally what *Wired* magazine recently said about technology and those who are creating it: "Let's face it. *We are gods and there is no stopping us.*"[4]

Kevin Kelly, writing in *Wired*, gives four reasons for thinking there is no stopping this economic surge:

1. *Demographic Peak*—The largest, best-educated, most prosperous generation that has ever lived is entering its peak years of productivity, earning, and spending. This is true not only for the United States, but also for much of the rest of the developed world. This boom of producers and consumers creates a huge market for purchases, a huge force of creativity, a huge pile of money, and a huge demand for investments.

2. *Technology Rush*—The largest deployment of novel products and services, labor-saving machines, and life-changing techniques

is now under way. In addition we'll begin to harvest the productivity gains of technology deployed in the last two decades. But most important, new technology is creating entirely new territories of economic development (the Internet and kin) that will be profitably settled in the next decade.

3. *Financial Revolution*—Money itself is undergoing a revolution. The velocity of money—how often it changes hands—continues to increase, middle-class values continue to spread around the world, and financial inventions continue to proliferate. Innovations such as mutual funds, rapid IPOs, microloans, 24-hour markets, hedge funds, smartcards, reverse auctions, and mass online trading liberate the flow of capital and spur intense economic growth. And the transformation of money and markets has only just begun.

4. *Global Openness*—The spread of democracy, open markets, freedom of speech, and consumer choice around the globe accelerate economic growth. Global openness not only enlarges the potential market, for any invention, to five billion customers (Red China), it also creates intense competition among governments to construct environments hospitable to progress. Prosperity can no longer be segregated to one part of the globe, and when prosperity does break out, it is amplified quickly by ever-spreading freedoms.

An impressive list of reasons that make the case for a prosperity that is just beginning, would you not agree? I read that list and was impressed. I think that what Kelly writes has much merit to it.

But he left two things out.

First, he left out God.

Second, he left out the sinfulness of man.

In essence, this writer is saying that we have reached a point where there is no stopping us. This has been said once before in history. That's what they said at the Tower of Babel. Perhaps you remember it. There was a concentrated effort of the entire world population at that time to pool their resources, their talents, and their gifts to build a tower that would reach up to the heavens.

And the LORD said, "Behold, they are one people, and they all have the same language. And this is what they began to do, and now nothing which they purpose to do will be impossible for them. Come, let Us go down and there confuse their language, that they may not understand one another's speech." So the LORD scattered them abroad from there over the face of the whole earth; and they stopped building the city. Therefore its name was called Babel, because there the LORD confused the language of the whole earth; and from there the LORD scattered them abroad over the face of the whole earth. (Gen. 11:6–9).

It's a big mistake to not "factor in" God.

For Judah, prosperity ended as swiftly as a grizzly moves on his prey.

Faster Than the Speed of Lightning

I have always been fascinated with grizzly bears. In my opinion, they are the animals of all the creation that should be feared most. When a grizzly sets his sights on you, there is no escape. Absolutely none.

My daughter spent some time this summer in Montana. When she returned, she told me that the section of Montana that she was in had more grizzly bears than any other. She did a lot of horseback riding up there. They would often see signs that grizzlies had been on the trail. Other riders reported seeing grizzlies. To use the biblical term, when she told me this, "my countenance changed."

I became very upset that my twenty-year-old daughter was riding horses in an area where grizzlies hung out.

"Who was in charge up there at that ranch!!!? What were they thinking!!!? Did anyone carry a rifle when you went riding in those areas!!!?" I asked in a soft, passive, and noncommittal tone of voice.

She informed me that none of the leaders carried weapons of any kind, even though they had lived in the area for years.

I couldn't believe my ears.

"How could they be so stupid not to carry weapons when they knew grizzlies were around!!???" I asked in a sweet spirit.

Rachel informed me that those wranglers aren't stupid. They are experienced.

"Dad, by the time you hear a grizzly coming, they are so fast that it is impossible to grab a rifle or draw a gun before they would be on top of you."

She was right.

What's the fastest dog in the world? A greyhound. Did you know that grizzlies are as fast as greyhounds?

When a grizzly charges, there are two words to describe them:

Rapid.

Sudden.

That's how judgment will come.

It will be rapid, and it will be sudden.

People who get mauled by grizzlies are usually taken by absolute surprise. They are hiking in the wilderness and they come upon a grizzly sow and her cubs. There is no warning. Many times there is no indication that danger is near.

But this is not true for us as believers. There are always indicators that judgment is on its way. And when it is about to hit with full force, there is always a sign.

It's called prosperity.

Wall Street on a Sunday Afternoon

Several months ago my son, Josh, and I spent a Sunday in New York City. I had been speaking that weekend at a Promise Keepers gathering, and we had just a brief time to see the city. So we decided to do a one-day blitz.

We started our tour at the Empire State Building. But just before we went in, Josh spotted a guy selling Rolex watches on the street. The price was a steal—only twenty dollars! So I bought one for him. When is a fourteen-year-old kid going to have a chance like that again? Then we got in line to go to the top of the Empire State Building. It took about an hour to get up there. But it was well worth the wait. It was a clear day, and you could see for miles.

Unfortunately, during the long wait Josh's new Rolex began to have problems. By the time we got to the top of the Empire State Building, the band just fell off his arm. What a rip-off. You'd think a Rolex would last a lot longer than that.

From that point it was a mad dash. We spent the day in and out of taxicabs. We took in Central Park, Madison Square Garden, and many other sights. Since it was Sunday, we decided to end our day by going over to the evening service at the Brooklyn Tabernacle. But on the way to the Brooklyn Bridge, I had the cabdriver take us one more place. "Where are we going, Dad?" Josh asked. "Oh, we're just going to a street. You'll see," I replied. Soon enough we were there. As we climbed out of the cab, I said, "This is it, Josh. This is the street. They call it Wall Street."

It was a very quiet Sunday afternoon. Just a few people walking around. In fact there were more people selling T-shirts and pretzels than there were people to buy them. Wall Street is a very small area.

But as Josh and I looked around and saw the impressive buildings, some that had been there for two hundred years, I explained something to him. I told him that we were standing on one of the most powerful pieces of real estate on earth. I explained that this was the very seat of financial power for the whole world . . . that the entire world watches Wall Street to take their cues from what goes on here. Josh took all this in on that quiet Sunday afternoon.

Wall Street is like that Rolex watch we bought earlier that day. What those street vendors were selling were obviously not genuine Rolexes. A genuine Rolex costs anywhere from five thousand dollars up. A real Rolex is hand-carved out of a block of solid gold.

But the imitation Rolexes are amazing copies. They look like the real thing. They would fool anyone who sees you wearing it on the street. That's how good they look. When Josh put on his Rolex, he looked like any normal fourteen-year-old with a Rolex. But eventually they are found out. A real Rolex will go one hundred years without breaking. But a counterfeit won't last thirty minutes.

People who trust in Wall Street to keep our economy strong are trusting in a counterfeit. Those who think that the prosperity we are enjoying will go on and on because of the power of the stock market are going to be as shocked as someone who bought a counterfeit Rolex thinking it was the real thing. Wouldn't it be a shock to lay down ten thousand dollars for a Rolex only to find it was a twenty-dollar counterfeit?

In the next chapter we are going to go much deeper to discover the wisdom of God on the issue of money. But for now, look at what the writer of Psalm 49 had to say about those who trust in their riches:

Why should I fear in days of adversity,
When the iniquity of my foes surrounds me,
Even those who trust in their wealth,
And boast in the abundance of their riches? . . .
For he sees that even wise men die;
The stupid and the senseless alike perish,
And leave their wealth to others.
Their inner thought is, that their houses are forever,
And their dwelling places to all generations;
They have called their lands after their own names. (vv. 5–6, 10–11)

Riches always come to an end. Always.

But God's grace is *unending*.

His mercies endure forever.

Do you find yourself feeling like Josiah? Do you see the false security of your life and the lives of those around you? Is your heart empty, in need of God's Spirit to fill you and change you? God heard Josiah's cry. And He will hear yours. "The eyes of the LORD move to and fro throughout the earth that He may strongly support those whose heart is completely His" (2 Chron. 16:9).

Give your heart to Him. Give it to Him fully. Completely.

Don't hold back your bank account.

Don't hold back your secret sin.

Give Him everything.

Give Him your mind, your soul, your spirit, just as Josiah did.

Ask Him to soften your heart. To make it pliable, humble, ready to obey. Ask Him to give you whatever you need to do the right thing in an evil day.

Just this morning I woke up early with a specific person on my mind.

A number of months ago I had a disagreement with this person over the telephone. I have not had any contact with this Christian friend since that phone call.

But I woke up this morning under the conviction of the Holy Spirit.

I needed to call the individual and ask his forgiveness.

My first response to the Spirit's conviction was to remind myself of where the other person had been at fault. But I had to immediately deal with that wrong response. It was not my job this morning to remind God Almighty of the details and circumstances of the conversation.

It was my responsibility to obey God.

So I did. I made the call. I admitted my sin and asked the forgiveness of my friend.

I'm so glad that I did.

Do you want to avoid a heart that becomes hard as a result of living in a prosperous nation? The next time God's Spirit convicts you, deal with it! Obey! Don't hesitate! Respond immediately to the prompting of the Holy Spirit!

That's what Josiah did.

May we follow the wide swath of his godly example.

5

1929 ALL OVER AGAIN?

The fate of the world economy is now totally dependent on the growth of the U.S. economy, which is dependent on the stock market, whose growth is dependent on fifty stocks, half of which have never reported any earnings.

**—Paul Volcker, former chairman of
the Federal Reserve; May 21, 1999**

WHAT AN AMAZING time to be alive!

The president of the United States is accused of an illicit sexual relationship with a girl young enough to be his daughter. Illegal drugs are easily found anywhere in America . . . from the largest of cities to the smallest of towns. The nation is stunned as two teenage boys go on a murderous rampage. A frustrated investor kills and wounds a number of innocent people at a stock brokerage office.

The 1990s?

No. The 1920s.

The president was Warren Harding. The drug was alcohol. To the shock of the nation, two brothers did the unthinkable. They murdered their parents. And someone who had suffered massive losses planted a bomb at a Wall Street brokerage house.

All of this was beyond belief. This kind of behavior sent shock waves through America in the twenties.

Then, on October 29, 1929, the stock market collapsed with a crash that was heard around the world. More than sixteen million shares were traded at a loss of ten billion dollars—twice the amount of currency in the entire country at that time.

The similarities between the 1990s and the 1920s are actually quite remarkable. The twenties were a time of economic euphoria. Business was booming. People were making money hand over fist. America's supremacy was felt around the world. And the moral and spiritual climate was in serious decline.

The decade of the twenties became known as the decade of decadence. At least three developments brought on this moral decline: the car, the radio, and motion pictures.

The widespread production of cheap automobiles first introduced by Henry Ford vastly improved the mobility of people previously dependent on urban mass transportation; the commercial development of radio greatly increased the power of mass communication, once limited to urban newspapers; and the moving picture camera spawned a huge industry that immensely influenced the mass culture that had first developed in the previous century.

Through the radio the siren call of the saxophone beckoned the young in the back parlors and small town cafes to jump in their roadsters and head for a speakeasy or a blind pig in the city. On the silver screen, Gloria Swanson, Clara Bow, Rudolph Valentino, and Douglas Fairbanks showed them how to act once they got there. The car, the radio, and the picture show broke down the isolation of rural life and dispelled the claustrophobic atmosphere of Main Street culture, precipitating the decline of small towns and the depopulation of the rural countryside.[1]

The car, the radio, and the movies brought about unprecedented change to homes of America. Before the advent of these three developments, people pretty much stayed close to home. Their entertainment was conversation after dinner or a really good book. But now they could listen to the radio. And they could get in their Fords and go into town for a movie.

Think of how the Internet has so rapidly changed American society in the nineties. Five years ago, if you had given someone an address with *www.com* in it, they would have looked at you as if you were an alien. Now just about everyone knows about *www.com*.

If you're on the Internet, you can go to a search engine and type in a topic. Within seconds a number of websites will come up on your screen. Click on the desired website, and in the time it takes to drink a sip of coffee, you are there. You can shop at L.L. Bean from your computer, you can visit the Library of Congress, you can check the baseball scores, or you can access any one of hundreds of thousands of pornographic websites.

Does a nation change when pornography can invade a home within a matter of seconds? You bet it does. Respectable men and women can now participate in sexual perversion without walking out the doors of their homes. And one visit to a pornographic website can undo years of moral teaching on the part of the parents. Kids are becoming sex addicts at the age of ten because of the Internet.

What the Internet has done in the nineties, the car, radio, and movies combined to do in the twenties. David Wilkerson summarizes well the decline of America in the twenties:

In a single ten-year period, from 1919 to 1929, America changed from a society of mostly religious, well-mannered citizens to a nation saturated with drunkenness, licentiousness and obsession with sex . . . Up to that time, most cars had no tops. But with the advent of the enclosed car came a sexual revolution. Unmarried couples started using their newfound privacy for sex. This moral upheaval prompted the newspapers of the time to label the new cars "brothels on wheels."

In retrospect, it's easy to be amused by the eroding morals of the twenties. Preachers of the time denounced women who wore rouge, calling them "painted ladies." They even cried out against women who bobbed their hair or rode bicycles on Sunday. But in truth, the acceleration of bad manners and morals in the twenties was no laughing matter. Suddenly, the upright morality of the past was being mocked—and the result was disastrous.

Soon, an obsession with sex swept the nation like wildfire. The subject became a daily focus of conversation. Sex-centered Freudian philosophy swept the land, and religious convictions about sex were ridiculed. Public dancing became sensual and intimate, and sex in movies and magazines grew permissive by the period's standards. (There was even some nudity in films and publications of the time, before the censor codes were put into place.)

. . . The situation was rapidly getting worse. By 1923, young women were crowding into bars during cocktail hour, just like men—hiking their feet up on the bar rail, getting drunk, and having to be carried out to their cars. And along with strong drink came even stronger words. Language suddenly turned foul and indecent. God's name was cursed everywhere, an act unthinkable just a few years before.

Not surprisingly, the standards and codes of marriage began to break down. Chastity and faithfulness grew outdated, and adultery became vogue. Over time, the new sexual immorality broke up homes all across the country. In 1910, almost nine marriages out of one hundred ended in divorce. By 1920, that percentage had risen to more than thirteen, and by 1928 it ballooned to one in six marriages.

Such drastic changes are hard to fathom, even by today's standards. Yet they all happened in just a few short years.[2]

Quite frankly, the newfound prosperity took the hearts of many away from God and all that they had been taught in their homes. The lure of the "good life" was incredibly strong.

Historian Paul Johnson, in his excellent book *Modern Times*, writes: "The truth is the Twenties was the most fortunate decade in American history, even more fortunate than the equally prosperous 1950s decade."[3]

In a very brief period of time, a nation that had been built on the principles of the Word of God began to fall into rapid and serious decline. As prosperity was increasing, spirituality was decreasing. America forgot who was making the prosperity possible, and they refused to honor Him as God. They forgot the warning God gave to Israel about prosperity:

Beware lest you forget the LORD your God by not keeping His commandments and His ordinances and His statutes which I am commanding you today; lest, when you have eaten and are satisfied, and have built good houses and lived in them, and when your herds and your flocks multiply, and your silver and gold multiply, and all that you have multiplies, then your heart becomes proud, and you forget the LORD your God who brought you out from the land of Egypt, out of the house of slavery.

He led you through the great and terrible wilderness, with its fiery serpents and scorpions and thirsty ground where there was no water; He brought water for you out of the rock of flint. In the wilderness He fed you manna which your fathers did not know, that He might humble you and that He might test you, to do good for you in the end.

Otherwise, you may say in your heart, "My power and the strength of my hand made me this wealth." But you shall remember the LORD your God, for it He who is giving you power to make wealth. (Deut. 8:11–18)

As I write this in the midst of a booming stock market, it's hard to believe that hard times could make another curtain call.

But my purpose in this chapter is to demonstrate that God could very well be setting us up to experience economic judgment, just as He did in the 1920s. God alone knows the future, but the similarities are more than striking.

One thing is certain. The crash of 1929 was not a random or isolated economic event. There were spiritual issues also at work. Greed had become acceptable. Speculation in stocks became so extreme it could have been equated to rolling the dice in Las Vegas.

Before the stock market crashed, spiritual and moral values had crashed. It's what you now may recognize as "cause and effect."

And these same issues are with us today, just as they were prior to 1929.

Arnold Toynbee, the eminent historian, wrote these words:

Our present Western outlook on history is an extraordinarily contradictory one. While our historical horizon has been expanding vastly in both the space dimension and the time dimension, our historical vision—what we actually do see, in contrast to what we now could see if we chose—has been contracting rapidly to the narrow field of what a horse sees between its blinkers or what a submarine commander sees through his periscope.[4]

The horse and the captain both are confined to very narrow perspectives. History widens the perspective. So let's go back in history to before 1929 and see what we can find.

www.tulip.com

In 1634, Amsterdam, Holland, was the financial capital of the world. Investors in Amsterdam were taken with a flower that had recently been imported from Turkey. This bulb, which looked like an onion, formed a tulip. Until then, tulips had been unknown in Holland. But tulips became the "Internet stocks" of 1634. This wasn't a Beanie Baby craze—this was serious business. Speculation on tulips swept Holland. Tulips became the commodity of choice for speculative trading and quick profit taking.

In the conditions of the seventeenth century, tulips were a preferred rarity for speculative trade. For one thing, the bulbs were smaller and more easily transported than porcelain or paintings. For another, they could be traded like coins or tokens in a futures market . . . During the height of tulipmania, in November 1636, single bulbs sold for prices equal to ten year's wages of the average worker.[5]

Translated into modern equivalent prices, this means that one tulip, just *one*, would sell for approximately four hundred thousand dollars! That's crazy! But is it any different from the inflated prices that people are paying for Internet stocks that have never made a profit?

The problem with these overvalued speculations is that they eventually come crashing down. It always happens. These inflated prices come crashing down in a moment's notice. Sure enough, tulips suddenly nose-dived. Investors lost 90 percent. And many people who had jumped on the bandwagon, thinking there was no end to this prosperity, were wiped out.

That was nearly four hundred years ago! But such frenzied speculation wasn't a onetime occurrence. It happened again in the 1700s in both France and England. France was burned by the "Mississippi Scheme," and England was flattened when the "South Sea Bubble" popped.

The point is this. It is a fact of history that empires rise and fall. And so do economies. *Especially economies that are experiencing such a boom that people think they won't fall.*

Solomon put it this way in Ecclesiastes 3:1–8:

There is an appointed time for everything. And there is a time for every event under heaven—
A time to give birth, and a time to die;
A time to plant, and a time to uproot what is planted.
A time to kill, and a time to heal;
A time to tear down, and a time to build up.

A time to weep, and a time to laugh;

A time to mourn, and a time to dance.

A time to throw stones, and a time to gather stones;

A time to embrace, and a time to shun embracing.

A time to search, and a time to give up as lost;

A time to keep, and a time to throw away.

A time to tear apart, and a time to sew together;

A time to be silent, and a time to speak.

A time to love, and a time to hate;

A time for war, and a time for peace.

Now Solomon didn't say: "A time for the economy to go up, and a time for the economy to go down."

But it sure fits his point.

To those who are saying that this economy is different from any other economy in history, Solomon has a response: "There is nothing new under the sun." In fact, note Solomon's entire statement: "That which has been is that which will be, / And that which has been done is that which will be done. / So, there is nothing new under the sun" (Eccl. 1:9).

In other words, if you want to know what is going to happen, look back and see what has already happened. As Winston Churchill put it: "The further backward you look, the further forward you are likely to see."

Lessons from the '29 Crash

It would be to our advantage to learn from the 1920s.

John Kenneth Galbraith was for many years professor of economics at Harvard. In 1954 he wrote the best-selling book, *The*

Great Crash of 1929. In his book, recently summarized in England by the *Financial Times,* he gives the following introduction:

> The pages which follow tell of the greatest cycle of speculative boom and collapse in modern times—since, in fact, the South Sea Bubble. There is merit in keeping alive the memory of those days. For it is neither public regulation nor the improving moral tone of corporate promoters, brokers, customer's men, market operators, bankers, and mutual fund managers which prevents these recurrent outbreaks and their aftermath. It is the recollection of how, on some past occasion, *illusion replaced reality and people got rimmed* (emphasis mine).[6]

Illusion replaced reality.

This describes the American mind-set in 1929.

It is also the American mind-set as I write in 1999.

There are three traits of the '29 crash worthy of note.

Trait #1:
The desire to "get rich quickly" began to sweep through the land.

The 1920s were years of tremendous prosperity.

> Productions and employment were high and rising. Wages were not going up much, but prices were stable. Although many people were still very poor, more people were comfortably well-off, well-to-do, or richer than ever before . . . [and many Americans] were *displaying an inordinate desire to get rich quickly with a minimum of physical effort.*[7]

In the mid-twenties, the average American had a good income and a steady job. Instead of riding a horse like his father, he had a new Ford in the driveway. He could take his wife out for a nice din-

ner and buy his children new school clothes. The economic outlook was positive, and there were no dark clouds in sight. Things
were getting better and better. The devastation of World War I was
over, and optimism was in the air.

In 1923 the stock market started to pick up momentum. By 1928
the average American was intoxicated by the gin of prosperity. The
promise of more and more was being offered through remarkable
gains in the stock market. Everyone wanted a piece of the action.
From the shoe-shine boy on the street to the president of the bank,
you could find them all in the market.

Trait #2:
The stock market became central to American life.

In 1927 the "speculative boom" began in earnest, with the bulls
far outnumbering the bears. A bull is an optimist who bets that
stocks will go up. A bear is a pessimist who bets that stocks will go
down. "Just as the ancient Israelites worshipped the golden calf, so
now thousands upon thousands of Americans worshipped the
golden bull of easy wealth."[8]

Galbraith makes the following statement about American life in
1929: "The striking thing about the stock market speculation of
1929 was not the massiveness of the participation. Rather it was the
way *it became central to the culture*" (emphasis mine).[9]

The stock market became central to the culture. Just like today.

It was central because so many Americans had a vested interest
in its success or failure. And it was central because it had now
become the yardstick for measuring our well-being as a nation.

When Christian men got up in the morning, many of them no
longer reached for their Bibles. The first thing they reached for
was the stock report in the paper.

Let me ask you a question. What happens when we begin to think about money first? The answer is simple. We lose our first love and our hearts grow very cold.

Jesus said:

No one can serve two masters; for either he will hate the one and love the other, or he will hold to one and despise the other. You cannot serve God and mammon . . . For all these things the Gentiles eagerly seek . . . But [continually] seek first His kingdom and His righteousness; and all these things shall be added [or provided] to you. (Matt. 6:24, 32–33)

It is impossible to seek wealth and seek God at the same time. We can only seek one or the other. What are you seeking? If you are seeking Him first, then you will eventually have to make some tough choices in life. Some of those choices involve saying "no." And some of those choices involve saying "yes." There are two things the world can't pass up: fame and prosperity. If you pass up either one, you qualify for the loony farm.

But Jesus says that if you seek His kingdom first, you are anything but crazy. In fact, you are thinking very clearly. A man who loves God rather than riches, and says no to the wrong kind of opportunity, is a man who has actually said yes. He has said yes to his wife and kids. And he has said yes to God's promise, or guarantee, that his financial and physical needs will be met (Matt. 6:33). How many people do you know who have that kind of financial security?

Seeking Him first keeps your feet on the ground while others are planting their feet firmly in midair.

Trait #3:
Risky speculation became the investment of choice.

"Early in 1928, the nature of the boom changed . . . *The time had come, as in all periods of speculation, when men sought not to be persuaded of the reality of things but to find excuses for escaping into the new world of fantasy.*"[10]

Americans were buying record numbers of stocks "on margin." "Margin buying" is a method of buying stocks by only putting 10 percent down. Your broker loans you the other 90 percent. With one thousand dollars in your brokerage account, you can control ten thousand dollars worth of stocks. All goes well if the market goes up and up. But if the market falls you could stand to lose ten times what you actually put in.

In the 1920s this kind of speculation was the name of the game—just like tulips in Holland and Internet stocks today.

The amount of speculation was rising very fast in 1928. Early in the twenties . . . [brokers' loans] varied from a billion to a billion and a half dollars. By early 1926, they had increased to two and a half billion dollars and remained at about that level for most of the year. During 1927, there was another increase of about a billion dollars, and at the end of the year they [had reached] $3,480,780,000. This was an incredible sum, but it was only the beginning. In the two dull winter months of 1928, there was a small decline and then expansion began in earnest. Brokers' loans reached four billion on the first of June 1928, five billion on the first of November, and by the end of the year they were well along to six billion. Never had there been anything like it before.[11]

According to Galbraith, "Especially after June 1 [1929], all hesitation disappeared. *Never before or since have so many become so wondrously, so effortlessly, and so quickly rich.*"[12]

Five months later it was all gone.

Americans thought, as so many think today, that it would never end.

But it did. And it eventually will.

History teaches that it will.

Professor Galbraith sums up his conclusion: "No one, wise or unwise, knew or now knows when depressions are due or overdue. Rather, it was simply that a roaring boom was in progress in the stock market and like all booms, *it had to end.*"[13]

On October 29, 1929, the unthinkable happened. The market collapsed. And the Great Depression was officially upon America.

Could we be in for another round of economic judgment?

Consider the following and then decide for yourself.

There's No Stopping This Market!

In the current American economy, as I write, people are making unprecedented profits. A recent cover story of *Newsweek* pictures a frustrated man on the cover asking, "How come everyone is getting rich except me?" The thrust of the story is that there are more new millionaires right now than at any other time in our history.

So what is funding this longest running wave of prosperity in American history? The stock market is driving it.

"The market not only moves up and up and up, but also as more Americans own stock . . . the rising tide is lifting a lot of boats, as well as hopes and dreams of short, profitable careers."[14] *The average*

American thinks that this prosperity is just getting started. A recent survey of investors indicated that they expect an average annual return on their stocks of 34 percent over the next ten years.

That's crazy.

It's mania.

It's also greedy.

Colossians 3:5 comes to mind: "Therefore consider the members of your earthly body as dead to immorality, impurity, passion, evil desire, *and greed, which amounts to idolatry*" (emphasis mine).

We are too sophisticated in this nation to bow down to idols.

We just crawl on our hands and knees down Wall Street, kissing the sacred pavement, unashamedly craving more.

This prosperity is so widespread and habit-forming that it is addicting college students even before they graduate. Sixty-one percent of college students think they will retire between ages forty and fifty. Seventy-seven percent of those same college students think that they will become millionaires.[15]

Talk to these college students about hard times, and they will reply, "Hard times? What hard times?"

The youth of America have joined the mania. It's too bad they haven't read the classic investment book *Extraordinary Popular Delusions and the Madness of Crowds*, by Charles Mackey:

> We find that whole communities suddenly fix their minds upon one subject and go mad in its pursuit; that millions of people become simultaneously impressed with one delusion and run after it . . . Sober nations have all at once become desperate gamblers, and risk almost their existence upon the turn of a piece of paper . . . Men, it has been well said, think in herds . . . They go mad in herds, while they recover their senses slowly and one by one.[16]

But history and the laws of economics tell us that markets go up and markets go down.

What Goes Up Always Comes Down

Donald L. Cassidy, a cum laude graduate of the Wharton School of Finance at the University of Pennsylvania, writes:

We know from even a casual glance at any long-term historical chart that stock prices do not move up in an uninterrupted straight line. In the twentieth century, stocks rose in about 7 out of 10 years—unfortunately, not exactly in 7 out of ten years. Would that investing were that simple. *Stock prices have declined by 10 percent or more, using the major averages as a measure, some 53 times, or on average one time per two years—but again,* not exactly once in each two years . . .

Another way of visualizing the data is to think in 12-year time windows: on average, such a span of years will contain four declines of 10% or more and another two of 25% or more.[17]

In other words, what goes up must come down. Always has, always will.

Dr. Kondratieff virtually proved it. So Stalin sent him to Siberia.

Dr. N. D. Kondratieff was a quiet, unassuming scholar. He loved to research, and he loved to teach. The long winters of his native Russia encouraged him to find a warm library and do his work. This man was not a revolutionary. He was not an anarchist. So why did he one day disappear, to spend the rest of his days in a Siberian gulag? Kondratieff came up with an economic theory that the Communist leadership did not appreciate.

Kondratieff taught that there are observable economic cycles of fifty to sixty years. In those long waves all kinds of things will happen. In those fifty years you will have a war or two, some inflation, multiple recessions, and usually at least one depression. But by the time the next wave rolls around, the new generation has forgotten about the previous wave. And they will think they are exempt from any economic downturn.

The Communists didn't appreciate Kondratieff's perspective. So they put him in a permanent deep freeze.[18]

In laymen's terms, Kondratieff was saying that what goes up must come down.

It's amazing how many American investors think that this market may have its moments of "correction," but that ultimately it will just keep going up.

A banker friend of mine recently told me about a client who came to see him about refinancing his business. My friend asked what his reason was for refinancing a business that was debt-free.

"To put the money in the stock market! There's no stopping this market!" the man said.

That's crazy. That's greedy.

It's also idolatry.

The banker turned him down.

Here was a once-rational man who wanted to take a business that he owned free and clear, mortgage it, and put the money into the market to speculate. Why would he do that? Because he doesn't know history. What goes up *must* come down.

What is presently fueling this sense of invincibility?

The question has to be asked: what is fueling record home sales, record car sales, record consumption, record debt?

The answer is simple. The bubble stock market has created false prosperity. Paper profits. People believe they can buy an Internet stock for $25 a share. Within a week it will go to $150 a share, split, then triple again. They will become wealthy.

They have no sense of value. No sense of earnings. No sense of risk. The U.S. stock market has become America's great casino.

This is not unusual. Bubble stock markets build and build until they make believers out of most everyone. Then, like a lightning bolt out of a clear blue sky, the market collapses.

We are now at the final stages of the greatest stock market bubble ever. All the signs are there. Huge volume. Absurd valuations. A mindless advance upward, that makes no economic sense. Promises of prosperity and riches, in a never-ending stock market boom (that can't possibly occur). These are the warning signs before every collapse.[19]

Larry Burkett has made an astonishing observation about the meteoric rise of this stock market:

Anyone who has money in the stock market today has to be astounded by its remarkable performance.

The market seems to defy all reason, especially in the case of Internet stocks. It seems that the more money an Internet company loses, the higher its stock soars.

It is a little advertised fact that the market in general is in a declining mode and has been for the past year.

*On the NASDAQ exchange, just 26 stocks have accounted for nearly 90%
of all the stock price increases.* The other 4,460 stocks show a net loss
of approximately minus 3%! *Even more amazing is the fact that 25 of
these top fliers have never made a profit.*

Even on the New York Stock Exchange, only 100 companies out of
the nearly 8,800 account for 92 percent of the gains. Other companies on the NYSE account for virtually no movement.[20]

This stock market growth is not only a bubble, it is an illusion.
When just twenty-six stocks account for 90 percent of the gains on
the NASDAQ, something is desperately out of kilter. And many of
these Internet stocks that have taken off like a rocket have *never*
made a profit. Yet they are driving the boom!

It's in times like these we've got to get a grip on ourselves.

It's in an economic boom that we must run the current trend of
thinking through the grid of Scripture. When we do, we find that
the world has turned things completely upside down.

Financial Advice from a Tent Maker

Paul was a tent maker, not a money changer. But he was uncanny
when it came to investments. He gave some great advice to a young
novice named Timothy:

But *godliness* actually is a means of great gain, when accompanied by
contentment. For we have brought nothing into the world, so we cannot take anything out of it either. And if we have food and covering,
with these we shall be content. But those who want to get rich fall

into temptation and a snare and many foolish and harmful desires which plunge men into ruin and destruction. For the love of money is a root of all sorts of evil, and some by longing for it have wandered away from the faith, and pierced themselves with many a pang. But flee from these things. (1 Tim. 6:6–11, emphasis mine)

Let me clear something up. God has commanded husbands to provide for their families. It's a heavy load to raise kids, pay the mortgage, and try to make ends meet. But that's your job. If you are providing for your family, then you are obeying God's command.

There is a big difference between wanting to adequately meet the needs of your family and desiring to get rich. Desiring to get rich is the snare that "plunges men into ruin and destruction."

How do you know if you have an unhealthy love of money? Paul gave us the answer. *If you are not genuinely content, then you have a problem.*

It's a very, very easy thing to fall prey to the subtle temptation to want more. There's a difference between needing more and wanting more. Your current job may not pay well. You may genuinely need more. But some people want more no matter how much they make. Needing more is not a lack of contentment. Wanting more is.

How to Lose Contentment in Ten Minutes or Less

Several years ago, on a hot summer afternoon, I fell right into the trap. Perhaps you have heard me tell the story before. But I think it bears repeating. I was worn out after mowing the yard for six hours in 100-degree weather and 90 percent humidity. So I sat down to guzzle another iced tea and bask in my accomplishment. I had to admit it. The yard looked like a million bucks and so did our ten-year-old house with its new coat of paint. As I took a sip of tea, I breathed deeply and thought to myself, "It's hot and I'm exhausted. But hey, life is good." A sense of contentment and satisfaction filled my heart.

That is, until I picked up one of Mary's magazines lying on the coffee table. As I flipped through the pages, I noticed an article about remodeling your kitchen. A couple from Des Moines had decided to redo their eleven-year-old kitchen, and when they were finished it looked, gosh . . . fantastic.

I flipped over a few pages to a do-it-yourself feature on putting a deck in your backyard. We already had a deck, but it didn't look anything like the deck in this magazine. Until now, I had been perfectly happy with the one I had. As a matter of fact, I had enjoyed it all afternoon when I took iced-tea breaks. It hadn't occurred to me until now that my deck was actually, well . . . embarrassing.

A few moments before, I had been filled with the all-American pride that comes with a sense of ownership and accomplishment. Suddenly, in a matter of moments, I could hardly stomach the idea of living in such a roach trap. *Just look at our kitchen! Those countertops are Formica! What we need to do is to get some countertops with ceramic tile,* I thought. *Why, we've got military personnel in Saudi Arabia eating in canvas mess halls that look better than this dump.*

And look at those rotting planks of wood that we call a deck! Why, I've seen firewood that's in better shape. What was I thinking, inviting the neighbors over to eat on that pile of junk?!

The sad thing is, I was fine till I picked up the magazine. By the way, can you guess the name of the magazine I was reading? It was *Homes and Gardens.* No, that's not quite right. It was *Better Homes and Gardens.* Better than whose? Better than mine!

Let me put it to you straight. The bug of *affluenza* has bitten me more times than I care to admit. And when that happens, if I don't make a 180 and run, I can get into some serious greed.

Listen to the rest of the tent maker's advice: "For the love of money is a root of all sorts of evil . . . But flee from these things, you man of God; and pursue righteousness, godliness, faith, love, perseverance and gentleness. Fight the good fight of faith" (1 Tim. 6:10–12).

In days such as ours, we must fight to keep our heads on straight.

And when temptation threatens to pull us in like a compass magnet to the north pole, we've got to grab our Nikes and head in the opposite direction.

Is it wrong to improve your financial position in life? Of course not. But you and I must realize that we have an enemy. And he knows how to bring us down. Money and prosperity are not simply economic issues. They are spiritual issues. And we must be very, very careful not to let them master us.

How should we handle our finances in these turbulent times?

As we look to the Bible, several principles come to mind:

1. *Don't spend what you don't have* (Prov. 13:22; 23:4–5).

We are making history right now. Economic history. For the first time in our history the average American is spending more than he is making.

The numbers are startling: The U.S. personal savings rate dropped into negative territory late last year and this past spring reached new record lows—minus 1 percent in March and April, and minus 1.2 percent in May. In other words, the average American each month is dipping into savings or going into debt in order to spend more than he earns. This is happening at the same time that incomes are rising; spending is simply rising faster. According to *Consumer Reports*, Americans are carrying debt equal to 99 percent of their annual disposable incomes. That's almost twice the level of 40 years ago.[21]

So if there is a crash of the economy, what is the average American going to fall back on? The answer is nothing. So make sure you can afford to lose what you are speculating. If you can't afford to lose it, then don't play with it. I have a couple of friends that have come up with a novel idea. They are speculating with some extra money that they have. But they have made a pact that whatever profits they realize will go directly into paying off the mortgage on the church building.

2. Decrease your debt, rather than increase it (Prov. 22:7).

This is a no-brainer. It's the economic equivalent to rolling up your car windows if it's raining. It's basic common sense. If you're not sure how to get started, contact Christian Financial Concepts or Crown Ministries. They can help you decide how and where to begin.

3. Invest in eternal things (2 Cor. 8:1–15).

Do you struggle with a desire to have more? Then give. Greedy people don't give. They hoard. Do you want to protect yourself from greed? Then increase what you are giving to your local church and other worthwhile ministries. It's hard to be greedy when you're giving sacrificially.

Giving toward those things that impact people for eternity is an immeasurably wise investment. The return on your money is exceptional. No earthly investment can touch it.

4. Invite the Lord Jesus Christ to be your primary financial adviser.

I'm sure that you have some trusted advisers to give you advice financially. And well you should. But the best advisers on earth don't know the future. And they don't always know the plans God has in mind for you.

Jesus desires to be the Lord of your finances and possessions. He has designed a portfolio specifically for you. So pray about your financial decisions and seek His wisdom. And when you pray, don't be double minded.

> But if any of you lacks wisdom, let him ask of God, who gives to all men generously and without reproach, and it will be given to him. But let him ask in faith without any doubting, for the one who doubts is like the surf of the sea driven and tossed by the wind. For let not that man expect that he will receive anything from the Lord, being a double-minded man, unstable in all his ways. (James 1:5–8)

When you pray about your finances, tell the Lord that you will do with your money whatever He asks you to do. A man who turns his money over to the Lord is a man who will be blessed.

5. Lean on the Lord as your primary provider.

There are times when the bottom drops out and our resources dry up. There are other times when we face decisions that are about as clear as mud or as tough as nails. At times like these you may need to do more than pray. You may need to fast. When you fast, you are momentarily setting aside the activities that fill and preoccupy your day, and you are devoting yourself fully to prayer without distraction. When a person prays and fasts and waits on the Lord, he is able to hear more clearly the voice of God. God speaks loudest in quiet places.

For many years of his life, David had no job. His employer, King Saul, had not only fired him, but he also wanted to kill him. It was during those years that David learned a valuable lesson:

Rest in the LORD and wait patiently for Him;
Do not fret because of him who prospers in his way . . .
For evildoers will be cut off,
But those who wait for the LORD, they will inherit the land . . .
Better is the little of the righteous
Than the abundance of many wicked.
For the arms of the wicked will be broken;
But *the LORD sustains the righteous* . . .
They will not be ashamed in the time of evil;
And *in the days of famine they will have abundance* . . .
The wicked borrows and does not pay back,
But the righteous is gracious and gives . . .
I have been young, and now I am old;
Yet I have not seen the righteous forsaken,
Or his descendants begging bread.
(Ps. 37:7, 9, 16–17, 19, 21, 25, emphasis mine)

The Lord *sustains* the righteous.
That was true in David's day.
It was true in 1929.
It is true today.
Our well-being and provision for our families are not based on what Wall Street does. They're based on what the God of the universe has promised to do.
If you need a better-paying job to meet the needs of your family, take it to the Lord.

If you're struggling with a job that has no challenge or opportunity to advance, bring that to Him as well.

He knows the pressures you face. He cares for you. And He promises to sustain you.

Don't lose heart. He knows where you are and what you need. His eye is upon you.

He took care of David.

He'll take care of you.

Some people have a piece of the rock; He is the Rock. The storms of economic adversity may indeed come, but the Rock stands secure. And so do you.

6

TIME OUT

When it gets very dark, then you can see the stars.

—Ralph Waldo Emerson

I'M OFFICIALLY CALLING a "time-out."

Sometimes calling a time-out is the only option left.

The team is down. The opponent is formidable. You've been out-played, outfoxed, outmaneuvered, outdone. And things don't look good.

At such a point, a good coach will call a time-out.

Time out for what?

For rest.

For perspective.

For reassurance.

For strategizing.

For regrouping.

That's why good coaches call time out. And that's why we've got to call time out.

There is actually such a thing as too much of a bad thing. An obvious statement? Sure. But in the American tough-it-out, you-can-handle-it mind-set, we can easily ignore the most basic of truths. We think we should be strong, that we should handle anything and everything. But we are only human, just like Habakkuk. The human heart can only handle so much bad news. "Hope deferred makes the heart sick, / But desire fulfilled is a tree of life" (Prov. 13:12).

Someone once said, "We can live forty days without food, eight days without water, and four minutes without air, but only a few seconds without hope."

If you and I are to survive physically, emotionally, and spiritually, we've got to have hope. Not false hope. Real hope.

That's what Habakkuk desperately needed.

And when we look honestly ahead, that's what we need.

Honest Hope

People have all kinds of hope.

There is the hope to win the lottery (unlikely).

There is the hope to lose twenty pounds (possible, but difficult).

There is the hope that God will always be there for you (true).

There is the hope that *hidden within* God's judgment will be certain blessing for the faithful (unexpectedly, but absolutely true).

But did you notice that little word *hidden*? Don't forget it. It's important.

Hidden Truth

At first I didn't see it. I couldn't see it. And then it became very clear.

My wife and I had just walked into an art gallery in Cannon Beach, Oregon. As we walked through the door, immediately in front of us we saw a very unique painting in only two colors: brown and white. It was a landscape scene of winter: brown grass, brown rocks on a hillside, all covered with a light dusting of snow. It is amazing how beautiful such a scene could be in just brown and white.

I took one step closer to move out of the doorway. And that's when I saw it! Actually there were two. There's another one! And one to the right!

Then Mary said, "Do you see the baby by her mother?"

What we suddenly saw—that we hadn't seen at first—were four camouflaged brown-and-white pinto horses. In fact, I have the print sitting in an open book on my desk as I write. I just pulled it off the shelf. I haven't looked at it in three or four years. I immediately saw the four adult pintos, but it was several seconds before I saw the little colt. They are so perfectly blended into the setting that I had to carefully look again to make sure I hadn't missed one.

When artist Bev Doolittle made the prints of *Pintos* available for sale in 1979, they cost $65. By 1989 they were going for $10,000. Who knows what they are worth today?

We have a book of her prints. Turning the page always presents a fresh challenge. And the challenge is to see what you don't see at first glance.

That's the way it is when we look at the judgment of God.

At first glance it is frightening and depressing.

The tendency is to lose all hope.

But you have to look again.

The hope is there.

It's just camouflaged against the background of the news of coming judgment.

Let me put it to you this way. Hidden truth is truth that is hidden only from our limited, immediate perspective. But it isn't hidden from God, the artist of history. In order to see it, we have to look from His perspective. And as we do, we discover something. Remarkably, God's viewpoint is more than true. It is also full of hope.

Firmly Planted in Midair

Habakkuk had just gotten some very bad news. And he was blown away. Knocked over. Blindsided. He had prayed for justice. He had asked God to act. He expected God to reply that He would bring down the evildoers and raise up the just. That's certainly what I hope for and expect when I pray for America. Don't you?

He expected God to say one thing. But God said another.

And from where Habakkuk was sitting, it looked like the worst possible news . . . news that he never in his wildest dreams would have expected.

Bad news comes to every one of us at some point in life. But it rarely comes when we expect it. Or in the way that we expect it. Sometimes it comes in the form of a phone call in the middle of the night. Sometimes it comes during a routine physical checkup. Sometimes it comes at a time of celebration, or just before a long-awaited promotion. That is the nature of bad news.

I'm sure that you've seen the roadrunner cartoons on TV. The roadrunner is always being chased by Wile E. Coyote. But the roadrunner is too smart to ever get caught by that coyote. Wile E. will spend hours laying the most intricate traps and ambushes in order to capture the roadrunner, but he always ends up being outsmarted by this bird, who can accelerate like a Corvette.

The classic scene is where Wile E. Coyote is chasing the road-runner, and the roadrunner is headed directly for a cliff. At the last second the roadrunner makes a sharp U-turn, but Wile E.'s speed keeps him from doing the same. His momentum carries him over the cliff, where he hangs in midair for several seconds. He realizes his mistake as he looks longingly back to the edge of the cliff. As he hangs in midair, his feet are going one hundred miles per hour in an attempt to get back on terra firma. But after several seconds he drops thousands of feet to the canyon below.

Habakkuk is like Wile E. Coyote. He can't believe what God is about to do. He has lost his footing, and he hangs in emotional midair. In an attempt to get back on land and get his feet underneath him, he does a very wise thing. I think he does it instinctively. I think Habakkuk had done it a hundred times before. And so it came naturally, spontaneously. I think as Habakkuk hung suspended over the Grand Canyon of despair, he instinctively did the one thing that saved him.

Habakkuk turned to the character of God.

It is always the character of God that gives us the perspective we need to get our feet back on the ground.

Mind Before Emotions

You've heard of mind over matter.

But have you ever heard of mind over emotions? Better yet, what about mind *before* emotions?

That's what Habakkuk did.

In the midst of emotional upheaval, Habakkuk began to *think*.

And these were his thoughts: "Art Thou not from everlasting, /

O LORD [Yahweh], my God [Elohim], my Holy One? / We will not die" (Hab. 1:12).

In these few brief, cascading thoughts, Habakkuk gives enough to think about for this entire chapter. In fact, his thoughts are so pregnant with meaning, we can only begin to touch upon them here.

Hang on with me while we try to do just that.

Eternal God

Habakkuk gathers himself and says, "Wait a minute, Lord. Aren't You from everlasting?"

The first thing that comes to his mind is the fact that God has always existed. He is everlasting.

What does this mean?

It means that God is eternal.

He has always been.

And He always will be.

There has never been a moment in time when God did not exist. As a matter of fact, He existed before time.

So when was God created? When did He begin? He never began. He was never born. He has always been.

So where did He come from?

He didn't come from anywhere.

He is.

And because He is, He is self-existent. He requires nothing and no one in order to exist as the complete and perfect everlasting God that He is.

This is a mind-stretching thought.

The psalmist tells us that He is from everlasting to everlasting.

Read these passages slowly and carefully:

LORD, Thou hast been our dwelling place in all generations.

Before the mountains were born,

Or Thou didst give birth to the earth and the world,

Even from everlasting to everlasting, Thou art God. (Ps. 90:1–2)

Of old Thou didst found the earth;

And the heavens are the work of Thy hands.

Even they will perish, but Thou dost endure;

And all of them will wear out like a garment;

Like clothing Thou wilt change them, and they will be changed.

But Thou art the same,

And Thy years will not come to an end. (Ps. 102:25–27)

J. I. Packer explains:

He exists forever; and He is always the same. He does not grow older. His life does not wax or wane. He does not gain new powers, nor lose those that He once had. He does not mature or develop. He does not get stronger, or weaker, or wiser, as time goes by. "He cannot change for the better," wrote A. W. Pink, "for he is already perfect; and being perfect, He cannot change for the worse" . . . God cannot cease to be what He is . . . such is the power of God's endless life (Heb. 7:16).[1]

God declares, "I am the first, I am also the last" (Isa. 48:12).

May I stop you right here for a moment?

Is it not true that for the last several seconds you have completely forgotten about judgment? We've been considering the self-existence of God. He has always been! He always will be! He had no beginning! He has no end!

Why should such a God, who needs no one and nothing, who is perfect in His eternality, consider you and me? Care about us? Love us with an infinite love? Give His own Son to save us? These are impenetrable questions with unfathomable answers.

When we turn to the character of God, it immediately begins to put our feet back on solid ground.

D. Martyn Lloyd-Jones considers this thought of Habakkuk against the backdrop of the distant sound of Babylon's marching feet:

> God is the eternal God, the everlasting God, from everlasting to everlasting. He is not like the gods whom people worship; he is not the god of the proud Chaldean army; he is God from eternity to eternity, the everlasting God. There is nothing more consoling or reassuring when oppressed by the problems of history, and when wondering what is to happen in the world, than to remember that *the God whom we worship is outside the flux of history. He has preceded history; he has created history* (emphasis mine).[2]

Our God is not only sovereign over history. He is also outside of history. He is the Creator of history. Every event—from the dropping of a sparrow to the destruction of a nation—is under His sovereign control and by His divine design. Every event.

The bottom line for Habakkuk was this: The destruction of Judah by the terrifying Babylonians was not the end of the world. It couldn't be the end, because God is eternal, and God had a plan for Judah.

All of this is expressed in Habakkuk's thoughts of the eternality of our God.

But let's move on to the next of Habakkuk's thoughts.

I AM WHO I AM: Yahweh

Habakkuk writes, "Art Thou not from everlasting, / O LORD? . . ."

If you have a modern translation of the Bible, you will notice that often the word *Lord* is written all in capital and small capital letters: LORD.

Whenever you see this, you know that this is a special word for the Lord. It comes from the Hebrew word *Yahweh*, the highest name given by the Hebrews to God, the name they never spoke aloud out of reverence for Him.

This was the name that God actually gave when He presented Himself to Moses in the burning bush. Moses asked God what he should say to the children of Israel when they asked who had sent him as their deliverer. "And God said to Moses, 'I AM WHO I AM'; and He said, 'Thus you shall say to the sons of Israel, "I AM has sent me to you"'" (Ex. 3:14).

It's the same name that Jesus used in referring to Himself as existing before Abraham. This so incensed the Pharisees that they tried to stone Him. He had equated Himself to God by saying, "Before Abraham was, I AM" (John 8:58 NKJV).

This name speaks of the self-existence and eternalness of God. But it means something more. It speaks of the eternal God who has revealed Himself to the world. It speaks of the great God who, being outside of history, had stepped *into* history, involving Himself in the affairs of men. This is Yahweh, the great "I AM," who chose the children of Israel, led them out of Egypt, and made the Deuteronomic covenant with them before they entered the Promised Land. The LORD, Yahweh, is so great that He is eternal, yet so personal that He cared about Habakkuk's thoughts at that moment.

Allow me to quote once again Lloyd-Jones on the meaning of the name Yahweh:

The most important and most significant name for us is the great name Yahweh (translated Jehovah in the AV). This, the Bible itself tells us, is the best name of all. It means that God describes Himself as I am that I am . . . The name describes, therefore, His unchangeableness, and especially His unchangeableness in His relationship to His people. Perhaps the best way to think of it is this . . .God is the self-existent One who nevertheless *does reveal Himself to His people* . . .

You find the Bible saying that this God has entered into covenants with His people . . . He promises, he covenants, to do certain things . . . This almighty being, whom we worship, who is self-existent in Himself, nevertheless *chooses to reveal and manifestly bind himself to mere creatures of time* like ourselves to those whom He has brought into being.[3]

When Habakkuk called out, "O LORD . . . ," he was calling out to the great I AM, who still involves Himself intimately in the affairs of mankind.

When you are hurting, and you think upon God's greatness, what a change it makes in your perspective when you remember this: The great "I AM" cares personally and deeply for you. He exists beyond the stars, yet He knows every hair that falls from your head and every tear that drops from your eyes. When you grieve, He is grieving with you. When you are confused, He doesn't laugh at your confusion. He is with you right there, arms around you, ready to take you, if need be *carry* you, safely through the fog. He is Yahweh, the God who makes and keeps His covenants and promises.

Just as a father has compassion on his children,
So the LORD [Yahweh] has compassion on those who fear Him.

For He Himself knows our frame;

He is mindful that we are but dust. (Ps. 103:13–14)

Elohim: All-Powerful God

God *holds history* in the palm of His hand as a man would hold an ant.

God *involves Himself in history*, as a father who cares deeply for his children, sticking with them through thick and thin.

And now Habakkuk's thoughts move to the fact that God is all-powerful. "Art thou not from everlasting, / O LORD [Yahweh], *my God [Elohim]? . . .*"

The term translated "God" here is *Elohim*. It means "Mighty God," and carries with it the idea of unlimited power and strength. It can also be translated "Rock," as in a mighty, massive, mountainous rock. Habakkuk could just as well have said "My Rock!"

He is reminding himself that his God, the Mighty One, the Rock, has unlimited power. There is no end to His power.

Consider with me the sun, which is more than a million times smaller than Betelgeuse, a red star in the constellation of Orion. Yet, as impotent as the sun is in comparison to many stars, its power staggers us. The energy it sends to earth alone is 126,000,000,000,000 (126 trillion) horsepower. Yet this vast amount of energy is only one two-billionth of the total energy sent out by the sun.

This, of course, is nothing before Elohim.

God has all power.

Let that thought sink in for a moment.

Why would God's power be so important to Habakkuk?

Consider the Babylonians. Consider their gruesome tactics in war. Consider their size. They were:

That fierce and impetuous people who march throughout the earth to seize dwelling places which are not theirs. They are dreaded and feared . . . [with horses] swifter than leopards and keener than wolves in the evening . . . They fly like an eagle swooping down to devour. All of them come for violence. Their horde of faces [literally, the eagerness of their faces] moves forward. They collect captives like sand. They mock at kings, and rulers are a laughing matter to them. (Hab. 1:6–10)

Now consider that this was the army coming to destroy Judah. Do you see why God's power mattered to Habakkuk?

What is the most fearful thing to you? Unemployment? Debilitating disease? The suffering or death of a child? The betrayal of trust by a loved one? Abandonment? Divorce? Perhaps you have begun to consider in these last chapters that America is not inpenetrable. America could fall. The judgment that God eventually brings upon us could even involve occupation or destruction by another nation more evil and godless than we. Christians the world over have faced just such terrifying situations, not just in previous centuries but in this very day. Thousands of Christians have died for their faith—this very year. When believers face such situations, what keeps them going? How does their faith survive? They trust in Elohim, the Rock, the One whose power is greater than any nation, any tyrant, anywhere on earth. They remember David's words: "God is our refuge and strength, / A very present help in trouble. / Therefore we will not fear, though the earth should change, / And though the mountains slip into the heart of the sea" (Ps. 46:1–2).

If they die, they face death not in their own strength, but in the strength of Elohim. And if they live, they live by His strength.

That's why, especially at our weakest moments, God says to us:

"My grace is sufficient for you, for power is perfected in weakness" (2 Cor. 12:9).

Habakkuk felt weak at the knees at the thought of the coming judgment upon Judah. And so he remembered God's power. Not simply for power's sake, but because God's power was a refuge for Habakkuk in the midst of the very worst life could bring. Habakkuk didn't have to be strong. He needed a strong God.

I want you to notice something. Suddenly Habakkuk has switched gears. He has moved from fearful awe to personal worship. Did you catch it? God is now "*my* Rock." In this moment of right thinking, Habakkuk has pulled close to God. God is his own personal God, the One to whom he has always clung in the past, and the One to whom he will cling right now.

Would God hold back the powerful army of Babylon? No. He would not. Babylon's army was coming at God's bequest!

Would God enable the faithful ones to come through those terrible days? Yes. A thousand times yes. Not because they were strong. But because He is strong.

Does God remove the things that threaten our undoing? Sometimes He does. But when He doesn't, He is the Mighty God, the Rock to whom we cling. And do you know what? He will bring us through it.

> I love Thee, O LORD, my strength.
> The LORD is my rock and my fortress and my deliverer,
> My God, my rock, in whom I take refuge; . . .
> As for God, His way is blameless;
> The word of the LORD is tried;
> He is a shield to all who take refuge in Him.
> For who is God, but the LORD?
> And who is a rock, except our God? (Ps. 18:1–2, 30–31)

The Holy One

Remember. Habakkuk is in midair. He's grabbing for solid ground. He remembers, God is eternal. God is personal. God is all-powerful.

And now, God is holy. "Art Thou not from everlasting, / O LORD [Yahweh], my God [Elohim], *my Holy One*?" (Hab. 1:12, emphasis mine).

Here is the significance of His calling to mind the holiness of God. Holiness is *absolute* purity and righteousness. This means that God, because of His holiness, purity, and righteousness can never sin or do anything that is wrong. In the next verse, Habakkuk expresses this: "Thine eyes are too pure to approve evil, / And Thou canst not look on wickedness with favor" (Hab. 1:13).

God is holy and utterly righteous. Therefore, if God thinks it best to send in the Babylonians to judge Judah, it is the *right* thing.

Whoa, as they say down here in Texas.

Stop right there.

This is important.

How many times have you heard someone say, "How could a merciful God allow bad things to happen?" Then they walk away. Case closed. There is no God.

But let's just back up. God is holy. Absolutely pure. He can do no sin. No evil. No wrong. The evil of this world is diametrically opposed to all that is the nature of God. So then, what do we say to this commonly raised question? We say this. Bad things happen because of sin. Sin has cursed the world. It has brought disease and death. And these touch us all. But when people sin (and we all do), we incur every manner of "bad things" upon ourselves—and everyone around us!

The questions we ask regarding God have to start with His holiness. The real question should be: How could a holy God provide forgiveness and salvation for such an evil world? Yet that is exactly what He did. That's because He *is* a merciful God. Our merciful God has provided a way out of our sin, through the substitutionary death of His own Son.

There is another question we should ask. This also begins with God's holiness: How could a holy God allow sin to go on unchecked? God's holiness requires justice. Many who raise the question of God's mercy are completely unconcerned with His justice. God's justice simply means that He always acts justly. Everybody wants a God who is fair and just. But if God is going to be just, He cannot allow sin to go unchecked.

Sin promises what it cannot deliver. It promises success, pleasure, happiness, and fulfillment. But instead it maims, destroys, and kills. And so, in His mercy *and* justice, the Holy One judges our sin.

Let me repeat that thought.

Judgment is an act of mercy, as much as it is an act of justice.

Is your mind stretching? Let it stretch a little more.

Do you remember our original statement at the beginning of this chapter?

The statement was this: *Hidden within God's judgment is certain blessing for the faithful.*

Could the judgment of God upon our nation actually bring benefits to us?

Is there an upside to judgment?

You bet there is.

The Wise Father

The eternal, strong, and holy God chose—no, let us be more accurate—*established* Babylon for the very purpose of judging Judah.

Without God's sovereign hand upon them, Babylon would have never risen to such power. But God raised them up to bring correction upon Judah.

You've heard of a midcourse correction.

That's what judgment is on a much larger scale.

It's the same thing that a parent does for a child who gets out of line and is disobedient. There is correction.

Severe judgment brings correction to a wicked nation. Habakkuk understood this:

> Art Thou not from everlasting,
> O LORD [Yahweh], my God [Elohim], my Holy One?
> We will not die.
> *Thou, O LORD, hast appointed them to judge;*
> *And Thou, O Rock, hast established them to correct.*
> (Hab. 1:12, emphasis mine)

There is an upside to judgment.

When God finally breaks the heart of a stubborn nation, changes can happen very quickly.

About one hundred years ago, there was a movement of God in Wales. People were called back to the Lord. Godless men and women were converted, and families were restored. As a result, profanity was virtually erased from the nation in a matter of weeks. The noted British preacher G. Campbell Morgan went to Wales to see what God was doing. He met the manager of a mine, who told him that this movement of God had actually caused some difficulty in the mines. The haulers, he explained, were men who were responsible for the donkeys and horses that pulled carts of ore in and out of the mine. Their morality and language had been of the rankest kind. They had always driven their horses with profanity and a whip. But now the horses were not responding to their commands. Why? Because the correction in these men's hearts had spilled over into a correction of their tongues. And since they no longer cursed, the poor animals were completely confused.[4]

The movement of God in Wales was a genuine revival.

But God corrects in ways other than revival. You and I tend to think that correction can only come through revival. But the judgment of America through the stock market crash of 1929 completely turned around the morality of the nation. In one fell swoop, the decadence of the twenties was replaced by the devotion of the thirties. And revival had nothing to do with it.

That's why there were benefits to the Great Depression. I read a book last year titled *Precious Memories*. This book was written by a number of adults who had gone through the depression as children. Without exception, every one of their memories was of the benefits that came into their lives due to the great correction that got the attention of a wandering nation.

Think with me for a moment. What benefits will come to us through the judgment of evil in this nation? We don't know how judgment will come. It may come in a *series* of judgments. But imagine with me a complete economic crash. There would be all sorts of hidden benefits to believers. Satan's primary wrecking tools would hit a major roadblock. It takes money to make filthy movies and CDs. It takes money to buy illegal drugs. It takes money to live in the fast lane. What would happen if parents and teenagers actually had to stay home and communicate with one another? Christian families might actually find themselves eating together and praying together more often. Neighbors might meet one another and form ongoing relationships.

We can think of any number of scenarios. What if we were to lose freedom, and democracy was replaced by tyranny—we are closer to this scenario than we might be willing to admit—and persecution of believers were to become a matter of course? What would happen to the fence-sitters, the "tares" of the body of Christ who simply *look* like wheat? What would happen to *your* faith?

Can you begin to fathom the hidden benefits to your life, to your family, to the body of Christ, should such a judgment be visited upon our land? The benefits are difficult to miss.

If difficulty and persecution were to come upon the body of Christ:

• Unbelievers would leave the church.

• Believers would be tested.

• Sin would be confessed and dealt with.

• We would become a people of prayer.

• We would pull together.

• Our Bibles would become the most important book in our lives.

• Children would bond to their parents.

• Thanksgiving would become more than a once-a-year turkey day.

• Believers would see the goodness and power of God in their lives as they have never before witnessed.

> Before I was afflicted I went astray,
> But now I keep Thy word . . .
> It is good for me that I was afflicted,

> That I may learn Thy statutes . . .
> I know, O LORD, that Thy judgments are righteous,
> And that in faithfulness Thou hast afflicted me.
> (Ps. 119:67, 71, 75)

Let's face it. Nobody in his right mind wants to experience economic disaster or tyranny or the spread of disease or any other kind of judgment. But if God determines that judgment is the right thing for America, then what a great thing it is to know that there is a definite benefit to that judgment.

Habakkuk's Question

Habakkuk has been thinking about the character of God.

He has realized that even if it means the destruction of Judah, God can be trusted. God knows what He is doing.

But a nagging question persists in his mind.

It bothers him so much that he can't get beyond it.

He begins his question with verse 13: "Why dost Thou look with favor / On those who deal treacherously?" (Hab. 1:13).

"Why, Lord," he asks, "would You use a nation *more evil* than Judah to bring us down? Why the Chaldeans, the most wicked people on the face of the earth? How can You, the Holy One, use such wicked instruments to do Your work?"

The more he thinks about it the more worked up he gets. How could this bring honor to God? How could righteousness prevail? "In fact," he goes on to say, "after these guys have captured us in their nets and devoured us, they will just sit back, burp, and gloat. Then they'll worship the very nets (made by their own hands) with which they have dragged us in. And after that, God, they'll empty those nets and go on slaying other nations! Lord, what will this have accomplished for Your name's sake?" (Hab. 1:14–17, my paraphrase).

I'm paraphrasing Habakkuk's words here, of course, but it's pretty close to the original.

It is as if Habakkuk is scolding the Lord. But his question is genuine. Habakkuk loved the Lord and wanted to see righteousness prevail. And so, in a subtle way, he is saying, "God, have You really thought this one through?"

I don't know about you, but if China or Iraq were to be God's tools of judgment on America, I think I would ask the same question. I've asked God that question regarding difficulties far less important in my life!

So what is God's response to Habakkuk's question?

Silence.

Absolute silence.

It was as if God left Habakkuk hanging there in midair.

When God Puts Us on Hold

Has your child ever asked you a question you didn't immediately answer? Has your child ever asked a question that you *couldn't* immediately answer—even though you knew the answer? If that is true between human fathers and sons, how much more is it true between our heavenly Father and His children! Not that He can't answer our questions—in His wisdom He *won't* answer our questions.

There are times when God allows us to remain suspended in midair, if you will. He lets us wrestle with things. Struggle. Sweat. Agonize. Work things through.

I hate when this happens.

No. That's not quite right.

I despise, detest, loathe, and abhor it.

So much so that I'll do just about anything to avoid it.

Unfortunately (and alternately very *fortunately*), God's in charge. And there's absolutely nothing I can do about it.

Sometimes God allows us to live in the tension of His silence for a while. Sometimes He lets us struggle as a butterfly struggles to break out of a cocoon and a baby struggles to take his first step. And as we do, something happens. The struggle builds muscle and provides new strength. Without the struggle, butterflies will not fly, babies will not walk, and we will not grow in our faith. Without the struggle, we will not come to know God as He wants us to know Him. Without the struggle, we will not come to trust Him as He wants us to trust Him.

Recently I ran across an article about NASA's research into the problems associated with space travel. I was fascinated by the fact that the most debilitating problem for the astronauts themselves is the danger that weightlessness poses to the human body. Without gravity we face life-threatening problems.

On earth, our bodies fight against gravity: Our muscles strain as we walk up stairs, and our bones maintain their strength to support the weight of our bodies. But at the earliest onset of weightlessness in space, an astronaut's body fluids—which on earth are drawn by gravity toward the feet—actually migrate toward the upper body. That's why when Neil Armstrong and Buzz Aldrin returned from their flight to the moon, their physical appearances had actually changed. Extra fluid had reduced their facial wrinkles and made their eyes look squinty and crafty. And with no gravity to compress their vertebrae, they had grown in height by about two inches.

But weightlessness affects more than our appearance. Without gravity the body mistakenly increases fluid in the thoracic region, and then initiates a complex process to get rid of it. The body thinks it has far too many red blood cells, so the bone marrow decides to quit producing bone marrow. Muscle atrophy is also another serious side effect, since the heart is a muscle. With no gravity to pump against, the heart grows lazy and shrinks in size. But scientists say that the most serious health problem is loss of bone density. In a state of weightlessness, the body gets rid of calcium, and bones lose density at one-half of 1 percent per month. Eventually, over time, the bones become brittle and break.[5]

The body's struggle against gravity turns out to be the very thing that keeps us growing and alive.

What do you do when God remains silent and allows you to struggle?

Once again, I think Habakkuk did something that was instinctively wise.

He climbed up to his guard post on the wall, high above the city. And there he waited for God's answer.

> I will stand on my guard post
> And station myself on the rampart;
> And I will keep watch to see what He will speak to me,
> And how I may reply *when I am reproved.*
> (Hab. 2:1, emphasis mine)

Why do you think he went up there on that post? Certainly he was watching and listening for the marching boots of the Babylonian army. But he was also listening for the voice of the Lord. Habakkuk knew that he had questioned God's wisdom, and he fully expected to be rightfully reproved. But Habakkuk was teachable. The reproof of God would be a welcome voice to his ears. So he sat there in the silence.

Watching. Waiting. Listening.

God's Answer

When God did answer Habakkuk, it was well worth the wait.

> Then the LORD answered me and said,
> "Record the vision
> And inscribe it on tablets,
> That the one who reads it may run.
> For the vision is yet for the appointed time;
> It hastens toward the goal, and it will not fail.
> Though it tarries, wait for it;
> For it will certainly come, it will not delay.
> Behold, as for the proud one,
> His soul is not right within him;
> *But the righteous will live by his faith.*
> (Hab. 2:2–4, emphasis mine)

God is about to give Habakkuk a vision of the far future. But first He delivers the rebuke Habakkuk had expected. If only I knew how to rebuke with such encouragement. Habakkuk's heart was not a proud heart. His spirit was teachable. He desired to understand and know the heart of God. And so God's rebuke was gentle and to the point: "The righteous will live by his faith."

In other words, "Habakkuk, there's a lot you can't see or understand right now. But stay close, stay obedient, and trust Me. Habakkuk, live by faith."

That was it.

I'll be honest with you.

When I'm struggling, that's not the kind of answer I'm looking for. I prefer not to walk by faith. My guess is that neither do you. We like to:

• Get all our ducks in a row.

• Be totally adequate for the demands of the day.

• Anticipate the future and be ready when it arrives.

• Pull ourselves completely together through times of crisis.

• Control our children's choices.

• Change the personalities of the problem people in our lives.

• Meet the needs of everyone else around us who is struggling.

• Understand all the answers to the questions that plague us.

God Wants Us to Live by Faith.

There is a well-known statement by Rabbi Simlai: "Moses gave Israel 613 commandments. David reduced them to eleven (Psalm 15), Micah to 3 (Micah 6:8), Isaiah to 2 (Isaiah 56:1), but Habakkuk to 1—"the righteous shall live by faith."[6]

Dr. Walter Kaiser points out that "Jewish scholars felt that these words—only three words in the Hebrew text—fairly summarized the message of the whole Bible."[7]

"The righteous (or just) man shall live by faith," is the bottom line of the Christian's life (Rom. 1:17; Gal. 3:11). We are saved by faith (Eph. 2:8–9). And now we walk by faith, trusting Christ to give us what we need (2 Cor. 5:7). Faith *pleases* God. "Without faith it is impossible to please Him, for he who comes to God must believe that He is, and that He is a rewarder of those who seek Him" (Heb. 11:6).

How foolish of me to think that I have what it takes to call the shots in my life. I've tried that before, and it always ends in failure. So God regularly puts me in situations where I have to trust Him. If He doesn't come through, I'm finished.

That's how Noah and Abraham lived. And that's how we've got to live. They trusted an unseen God in the seen events of life. And He rewarded them.

Faith is the assurance of things hoped for, the conviction of things not seen. For by it the men of old gained approval. By faith we understand that the worlds were prepared by the word of God, so that what is seen was not made out of things which are visible. By faith Abel . . . By faith Enoch . . . By faith Noah . . . Abraham . . . Sarah . . . Isaac . . . Jacob . . . Joseph . . . Moses . . . Rahab . . . Gideon . . . Barak, Samson, Jephthah, of David and Samuel and the prophets. (Heb. 11:1–32)

The list goes on. Someday we will get to meet every member in the Great Hall of Faith. And one of them will be Habakkuk.

The Just God

Finally God responds to Habakkuk's troubling question. Can God use unholy instruments to carry out His will?

Scripture is clear: He can and He often does. John Calvin once said, "When God wants to judge a nation, He gives them wicked rulers."

But never forget. What goes around comes around. The day would eventually come when the Babylonians would have their day in court. Throughout chapter 2, God pronounces a curse upon Babylon:

Woe to him who builds a city with bloodshed
And founds a town with violence! . . .
The cup in the LORD's right hand will come around to you,
And utter disgrace will come upon your glory.
For the violence done to Lebanon will overwhelm you,
And the devastation of its beasts by which you terrified them,
Because of human bloodshed and violence done to the land,
To the town and all its inhabitants. (Hab. 2:12, 16–17)

What the Babylonians were about to do to Judah, the same would be done to them. Justice would prevail. And the Lord would be glorified (2:14, 20).

The Faithful God

Some of you have probably been wondering about something.

You may have noticed that I skipped over a phrase.

As Habakkuk contemplated the character of God, he said an interesting thing. Do you remember? "Art Thou not from everlasting, / O LORD, my God, my Holy One? / *We will not die*" (1:12, emphasis mine).

That's a strange thing for him to say, don't you think?

Why would he say, "We will not die," when he knew many of them *would* die?

Habakkuk was referring to the chosen people of God. God made a covenant with the children of Israel. He promised that they would never be completely wiped out. He promised that the Messiah of the world would come from among them. And He promised that even though Judah would be destroyed, its people would not be completely annihilated. One day, said the Lord through His prophets, Israel would be restored. Yahweh would once again be their God, and they would be His people. The prophets spoke clearly and in great detail about this. When they wrote about it, you could almost see them dancing with joy. What a day of blessing and joy it would be. The lion would lie down with the lamb. Their swords would be turned into plowshares. The rivers and springs would be full, and the fields rich with harvest. And the name of God would be lifted up and praised.

Has God kept that promise? In the days of Esther, the Jews were saved from complete annihilation. Time and again we have seen God's mercies upon the Jews. Hitler tried, but no man or nation will ever be able to annihilate the Jews. That's a guarantee.

But the day of Israel's restoration is yet to be fulfilled. That's why today the Jews stand at the Wailing Wall in Jerusalem, praying and waiting for the fulfillment of God's promise.

This is why Habakkuk said with confidence, "We will not die."

Can we say the same thing of America? God has not given any other nation this promise.

But He has pledged His faithfulness to those who belong to Him.

Quick. What is the most famous geyser in the world? Old Faithful. Old Faithful is never closed. It never needs repair. It never dries up. If you go to see it, you will never be disappointed.

Approximately every 65 minutes, Old Faithful will show you its stuff. It will shoot water up anywhere between 120 and 170 feet, and will do so for approximately 4 minutes. If you get there at the end of the show, be patient. Another performance will begin in

65 minutes. Seven days a week, twenty-four hours a day. Winter, spring, summer, or fall.

You can count on it.

You can count on Him. "Know therefore that the LORD your God, He is God, the faithful God, who keeps His covenant and His lovingkindness to a thousandth generation with those who love Him and keep His commandments" (Deut. 7:9).

The God of Joy

Though the old prophet began in a state of depression, he finishes in an attitude of rejoicing!

Note that Habakkuk's rejoicing doesn't ignore the difficulty that is coming. He knows what is coming:

> I heard and my inward parts trembled;
> At the sound my lips quivered.
> Decay enters my bones,
> And in my place I tremble.
> Because I must wait quietly for the day of distress,
> For the people to arise who will invade us. (3:16)

He still dreads the coming judgment. But Habakkuk has come full circle. He is going to describe the worst possible scenario that he could imagine. And then he rejoices. Amazing!

> Though the fig tree should not blossom,
> And there be no fruit on the vines,
> Though the yield of the olive should fail,
> And the fields produce no food,
> Though the flock should be cut off from the fold,
> And there be no cattle in the stalls,
> Yet I will exult in the LORD,

I will rejoice in the God of my salvation.
The Lord GOD is my strength,
And He has made my feet like hinds' feet,
And makes me walk on my high places. (3:17–19)

Isn't it amazing how thoughts of God can so totally change a man's perspective? This guy has come a long way in three chapters!

He started with anxiety, and now he is accepting.

He was paralyzed with fear, and now he is full of faith.

He was weak in the knees, and now he is rejoicing in God's strength.

He was sick with worry, and now he cannot help but worship.

His feet were in midair. But now they are like hinds' feet, firmly and securely planted on solid rock.

As the sound of the Babylonian troups could be heard in the distance, Habakkuk asked of God one final request: "O LORD, revive Thy work in the midst of the years, / In the midst of the years make it known; / In wrath remember mercy [or compassion]" (3:2).

Habakkuk was asking God not to forget the work He had promised to do through His chosen nation. He was asking God to revive Judah! And he was begging God to be merciful even in the midst of the well-deserved wrath that was about to be poured out on Judah.

Little could the old prophet have known that even as he prayed, God was answering that prayer.

Somewhere down below on the streets of Jerusalem was a young Jewish teenager who was destined to be carried off to Bablylon. But this young man was special because he was part of the remnant. And he loved the Lord with all his heart and soul and mind.

His name was Daniel.

And it's to Daniel that we turn.

7

DANIEL'S DIVINE DESTINY

Dare to be a Daniel,
Dare to stand alone!
Dare to have a purpose firm!
Dare to make it known!

—**Philip P. Bliss**

IMAGINE THE UNTHINKABLE. Imagine the economy of the United States in devastation and utter ruin. On top of that, imagine that we have been invaded by China. Picture—if you can—what it would be like as the Chinese People's Army skims off the very cream of the freshman class from West Point, Annapolis, and the Air Force Academy, and hauls them off to Beijing, never to return to America again.

That is unthinkable! We cannot comprehend what it would be like for us to have a foreign army on our shores and to watch them take our kids away to train them in the ways of their godless culture.

Yet that is exactly what happened to Daniel. He experienced all of that upheaval in his own life.

Daniel lived in Judah in a day of judgment. It would not be stretching things to suggest that perhaps his family were personal friends of Habakkuk. Daniel was just a teenager when Gods' righteous wrath fell upon Judah—that stubborn and rebellious nation. Daniel was neither rebellious nor hard-hearted; he loved and followed the Lord. Even so, this young man's long-range plans—all of his hopes, aspirations, and dreams for the future—took a direct, devastating hit. His life's game plan was interrupted. Yet God's game plan for Daniel was not interrupted at all. In the divine scheme of things, Daniel's sudden relocation to Babylon was right on schedule. Life would go on . . . it just wasn't going to be anything like Daniel thought it would be.

When we are young, we try to peer over the horizon and form a mental picture of what we think our lives will look like. We will finish school, get a job, find a mate, start a family, buy a house, get another car, have another child, put the kids through college, marry them off, adjust to the empty nest, and eventually retire at some point, play a little golf, and do some traveling. In our minds, that's the way life is supposed to go.

It seldom works out that way.

Especially if you are living in a time of judgment.

But let me reiterate that judgment on a nation does not interrupt God's plan for your life. Judgment *compliments* and *cooperates* with God's plan for your life. No judgment in the world can get in the way of what God wants to do for you, in you, and through you. Judgment is simply another tool in God's Swiss Army knife. God's dealings with the nation will not prevent Him from doing what is best for you.

You can count on that.

That is certainly what happened to Daniel. The judgment on Judah enabled Daniel to fulfill the destiny that God had designed for him before the foundations of the earth.

If the shadows of God's judgment fall across America, we will need to take our cues from Daniel. How do you live in a nation that is under the discipline of the Lord? How do you cope when life is turned completely upside down? Is there any hope? Will God continue to be faithful? Or are things so bad that there is no hope?

Whenever God has sent judgment in history, He has always kept a remnant for Himself. My wife has been looking for some new curtains. She came home the other days with some remnants. Remnants are small samples of fabric cut from the larger bolt. The remnant demonstrates what the larger bolt of cloth is supposed to look like. It's a small swatch of cloth, four or five inches in diameter.

Mary can look at that little sample of cloth and imagine what it will look like as curtains. I'm certainly glad she's gifted this way, because to me it looks more like a postage stamp than a new look for a living room.

God has an eye for remnants, too, and out of the entire rebellious nation of Judah, God had a remnant. They were small in number, but they represented what Judah should have been. They followed the Lord with their whole hearts. They were His people. They were faithful to the covenant. When judgment fell on the nation their lives were interrupted, yet God continued to be faithful to them and to look out for them.

Daniel was part of that remnant. So were his buddies Hananiah, Mishael, and Azariah (later known as Shadrach, Meshach, and Abed-nego). These four young men showed us that it is possible to live in the midst of judgment and still experience the blessing and favor of God. They demonstrated how to do it. We should watch them very, very carefully.

How Judgment Came

How did it come? Remember Josiah, the godly king who discovered the Book of the Law in the temple? When Josiah died, his youngest son, Jehoahaz, was put on the throne by Neco, pharaoh of Egypt. It was Neco who had fatally wounded Josiah in battle. Neco soon tired of Jehoahaz, however, and just a couple of years later, replaced him with his eldest brother, Jehoiakim. During Jehoiakim's third year on the throne it all started to come down:

> In the third year of the reign of Jehoiakim king of Judah, Nebuchadnezzar king of Babylon came to Jerusalem and besieged it. And the Lord gave Jehoiakim king of Judah into his hand, along with some of the vessels of the house of God; and he brought them to the land of Shinar, to the house of his god, and he brought the vessels into the treasury of his god. (Dan. 1:1–2)

So how did judgment finally come?

They were *delivered*.

They weren't delivered *from* Nebuchadnezzar, they were delivered *into* the hand of the Babylonian king.

Now you might look at this verse and say that they weren't delivered, they were defeated. It appears that way at first glance. But a closer look reveals that they weren't defeated, they were delivered, the same way that Fed Ex delivers an overnight letter to your front door. They were given to Nebuchadnezzar. It's not that

Nebuchadnezzar came in and after a long and bloody battle his army prevailed. No, it wasn't that way at all. God, as an act of judgment, just gave them to Nebuchadnezzar. He handed them over, and they were carried off to a foreign land. Why did He do that? Because He said He would do this if they failed to obey Him (Deut. 28:49–68). This was the final and worst judgment of all the curses. Judah wouldn't listen to Him. So it came to this.

Note that they were *drafted and deported*.

> Then the king ordered Ashpenaz, the chief of his officials, to bring in some of the sons of Israel, including some of the royal family and of the nobles, youths in whom was no defect, who were good-looking, showing intelligence in every branch of wisdom, endowed with understanding, and discerning knowledge, and who had ability for serving in the king's court. (Dan. 1:3–4)

My son, John, just turned eighteen a few months back. Last week he got a postcard from selective service. They instructed him to fill out the card and send it in because he is now eligible for the draft.

Nebuchadnezzar came in and held a draft. Only he didn't take everyone over eighteen. He just wanted the cream of the crop. He took the young teenage males who were the best athletes, the best scholars, guys who demonstrated a maturity beyond their years and the potential to be successful in future endeavors.

Now here is where we meet Daniel. Daniel was apparently part of the royal family. We don't have any more detail than that. He was born sometime during the reign of the godly king Josiah. He was around sixteen to eighteen years old when Nebuchadnezzar showed up. And this is when all of Daniel's plans for the future took a tremendous turn.

Daniel was not only drafted, he was deported.

Daniel, Hananiah, Mishael, and Azariah were carted off to Babylon. They were the equivalent of high school juniors or seniors.

There was probably very little time to say good-bye. As the intended captives were torn from their families to begin the long march, two visual images must have burned in their hearts: the anguish-filled faces of their loved ones, and that last glimpse of the city God had abandoned to its fate—beloved Jerusalem. A fleeting glance . . . and it was all behind them. They were on their way to a future filled with dark mysteries. Destination: Babylon.

Try to identify with the emotional upheaval—the wrenching inner pain—of these teenagers as they were swept along the ancient trade route with the conquering Babylonians. Feel the sorrow and remorse—the anger and fear that must have brought tears to their eyes and knots to their stomachs. Their homes, their families, their proud temple all behind them—perhaps forever. Familiar streets, familiar faces, best friends and sweethearts—gone! How powerless they must have felt. Judah's weak, shattered army could not help them. And ahead? A strange, alien city in a land so far away it might as well have been the moon. Would God actually allow them to live out their lives in that forbidding and foreboding city, rumored to be filled with bizarre temples and teeming idolatry? Unthinkable![1]

This was a shattering experience. Life as they had known it was over. But life as God intended was still on track. Daniel was headed in a strange direction, but God's protection and direction never left the young man's shoulders.

He must have felt the very same way that another teenager, Joseph, had felt when he was sold to the caravan heading for Egypt. But just as God had a plan for Joseph, so He had a plan for Daniel.

The great chemist Michael Faraday was away from his lab when an accident occurred. He had been given a silver cup years before. It was his favorite cup and had much sentimental value. He would usually have that silver cup full of tea that he would sip throughout the day. On this particular afternoon a lab assistant accidentally knocked the cup off the shelf and into a solution of acid that he was working with.

The assistant was horrified as he watched the acid dissolve the silver cup before his eyes. There was nothing he could do. When Faraday returned, the embarrassed man told him what had happened and began to apologize profusely. Faraday patted the assistant on the shoulder and went into his lab where he retrieved a powder. He poured the powder into the solution of acid, and within seconds the silver had accumulated at the bottom. He then removed the shapeless silver and took it to the silversmith from whom he had purchased the cup.

The lab assistant was shocked several weeks later to see Faraday sipping tea out of a cup identical to the one he had knocked into the acid. Faraday explained that it was the same silver cup. The silversmith had taken the shapeless mass and reworked it into its original form.

I'm sure Daniel and Joseph, as they were both forced to journey to a foreign land, felt that their lives had fallen into the acid of tragic circumstances. But unbeknownst to them, God was taking what they thought was loss and shaping it into great gain. It would be years, however, before they would understand this.

In a sense these young men were very fortunate. Life was brutal back then—and cheap. When one nation would defeat another nation, the victors would often kill all of the men, ravage the women, and install their own people to rule the land. The Babylonians didn't work that way.

They had a strategy of taking the young leaders—the best and the brightest—and changing them. They would change their address by deporting them and separating them from family and friends. They wanted to change them completely. They wanted them to forget their old ways and customs. They wanted to reprogram them, turning them into nationalized Babylonians. How did they try to change them?

The king ordered Ashpenaz, the chief of his officials, . . . and he ordered him to teach them the literature and language of the Chaldeans. And the king appointed for them a daily ration from the king's choice food and from the wine which he drank, and appointed that they should be educated three years, at the end of which they were to enter the king's personal service.

Now among them from the sons of Judah were Daniel, Hananiah, Mishael and Azariah. Then the commander of the officials assigned new names to them; and to Daniel he assigned the name Belteshazzar, to Hananiah Shadrach, to Mishael Meshach, and to Azariah Abednego. (Dan. 1:3–7)

Nebuchadnezzar, this Babylonian king, had a plan for these choice Jewish teenagers:

- He would change their curriculum.

- He would change their language.

- He would change their diet.

- He would change their education.

- He would change their names.

I recently read of a General Motors plant that was "retooling." They had been building Chevrolet Caprices. But everyone wanted Chevy Suburbans and Tahoes! So in order to meet the demand, they shut down the plant for a number of months and "retooled." That assembly line was going to have to change if it was going to turn out Suburbans instead of sedans.

That's what Nebuchadnezzar was going to do with Daniel and his friends. He was going to completely "retool" them. He was going to change them from Jews to Babylonians. But it wasn't going to happen overnight. It would take time. Intense time. Everything would be new, and everything would be different. He would force them to change, compromise, and concede. In *everything*.

Or they would die.

What an overwhelming situation for a young man to find himself in! How would you have coped with this at age sixteen or seventeen?

There is one ingredient that is absolutely necessary when forces around you are pressuring you to change, compromise, and concede. And this is the ingredient that allowed Daniel and his three amigos to survive.

They had *convictions*.

Convictions they wouldn't change.

Convictions they wouldn't compromise.

Convictions they wouldn't concede.

It's not that these young men rebelled against the whole program. In fact, they agreed to go along with most of the changes. They agreed to the change in curriculum. They were introduced to literature that they had never seen before. They read it, for the Scriptures did not prohibit doing so.

They agreed to learn a new language. After all, they were going to have to get along, and to do so, it only made sense to learn this new and difficult language.

They agreed to the three years of advanced education. This intense Ph.D. program "probably included a study of agriculture, architecture, astrology, astronomy, law, mathematics."[2]

They even agreed to the change in names. There was nothing biblical that prevented them from taking Babylonian names. After all, they were going to be a part of this culture.

But when it came to the matter of diet, they would not agree.

Diet?

What's the problem with diet? Why wouldn't they compromise on food?

There are a couple of possible explanations. The first is that they were very careful to observe the dietary restrictions that God had given in the Law. The second is that the meat offered to them as part of the king's table had first been offered to pagan idols as a sacrifice.

That's where they drew the line.

On this one they weren't going to change, compromise, or concede.

Why not?

Conviction.

"But Daniel made up his mind that he would not defile himself with the king's choice food or with the wine which he drank" (Dan. 1:8).

Daniel "made up his mind." The King James Version says that he "purposed in his heart." On this one, there was no turning back. Come what may, live or die, Daniel was drawing a line in the sand.

He could accommodate a name change, a change of his major, and even a new language. But on this one he wouldn't budge. They were asking him to violate a conviction. And that was something he wasn't willing to do.

Now apparently the other Jewish boys were willing to go along with the change in diet. But Daniel, Hananiah, Mishael, and Azariah wouldn't. What was the discrepancy? They were all Jews, and they had been taught the Word of God.

The difference is this: They all had beliefs, but Daniel and his friends had convictions.

Bruce Wilkinson hits the nail squarely on the head:

There is a vast difference between holding a belief and entering into a conviction. One is a matter of the intellect, the other a matter of the will. One says, "I am convinced." The other says, "I am committed." A man may argue for his beliefs, but he will die for his convictions. A belief is something that is held in the hand. If the pressure is great enough, if the storm is fierce enough, a belief may become dislodged from the grip and slip away in the current. A conviction, however, is held in the heart. It is stitched into the fabric of one's very being. No pressure, no storm—no matter how violent— can destroy a conviction without destroying something of the one who holds it. A conviction is nothing more than a belief with its boots on . . . ready to march, ready to fight, ready to die.[3]

It takes courage to be willing to die for a conviction.

Benjamin Franklin once said that "a man without courage is like a knife without an edge."

Having courage doesn't mean you don't have fear. In fact, you may be clearly afraid. Courage simply means you are ready to put yourself on the line in spite of fear. Courageous people know all about fear . . . they just don't allow the fear to control them. Their convictions control them.

Marshal Michel Ney was one of the bravest commanders in

Napoleon's army. Napoleon referred to him as the bravest man he had ever known. Yet as he got ready to lead his troops into a particular battle, his knees were shaking so badly that it was all he could do to get his foot in the stirrup and mount his horse. When he got into the saddle, he said, "Shake away, knees. If you knew where I was about to take you, you would shake even more."

Courage is not the absence of fear. It is doing what is right in spite of your fear.

It takes courage to stand up. And when standing up could cost you your life, it will only be the person of conviction who is willing to do so. This person is willing to die for what he believes.

The men who signed the Declaration of Independence were men of conviction. They were willing and ready to die. Did you know that the Declaration of Independence ends with the following statement: "For the support of this Declaration, with a firm reliance on the Protection of Divine Providence, we mutually pledge to each other our Lives, our Fortunes and our sacred Honor"?

These men were serious about their convictions. Deadly serious. These men put it all on the line. Their fortunes. Few men will risk anything that might affect them financially. These men put everything they owned on the line. Why? Conviction.

Daniel stood up.

Like Daniel they were outnumbered.

But like Daniel they stood up.

The colonies had no human chance of winning a war with England. The British Empire at that time possessed the most formidable fighting forces on the face of the earth. The ragtag assembly of volunteers, farmers, and tradesmen who composed the ranks of the American military were out-manned, out-gunned, out-financed, and out-generaled. Only a miracle could bring success in a war with Great Britain.[4]

Just as Daniel stood up, the signers of the Declaration of Independence stood up. On July 4, 1776, they signed their names to a document that could cost them everything. If they lost the war with Britain—and the odds were almost overwhelming that they would—they would lose everything . . . their freedom, their property, their fortunes, their families, and their lives. The vast majority of these men were Christians. Committed Christians. They were disciples of Jesus Christ. And that's why they stood against tyranny. You know about the Boston Tea Party. That was the night they decided to take the massive taxation of tea upon their shoulders no more. As a protest, they took the sacks of tea and poured them into the sea. But did you know that these men had such integrity that they actually paid for the tea that they dumped overboard?

What happened to those fifty-six men who signed that document?

Carter Braxton of Virginia, a wealthy planter and trader, saw his ships swept from the seas by the British Navy. To pay his debts he lost his home and all of his properties, and died in poverty.

Thomas Lynch, Jr., an aristocratic plantation owner, was a third-generation rice grower. After he signed, his health failed. With his wife he set out for France to regain his health. Their ship never reached France, and he was never heard from again.

Thomas McKean of Delaware was so harassed by the enemy that he and his family were forced into hiding, moving five times during the war. He served in Congress without pay. Poverty was his reward.

Vandals and enemy soldiers looted the properties of Bartlett, Ellery, Clymer, Hall, Gwinnett, Walton, Heyward, Rutledge, and Middleton. The latter four were captured and imprisoned.

Thomas Nelson, Jr., of Virginia, raised two million dollars to supply our French allies by offering his property as collateral. Because he was never reimbursed by the struggling new government, he was unable to repay the note when it came due—wiping out his entire estate. In the final battle for Yorktown, Nelson urged General Washington to fire on Nelson's family home, as it was occupied by the British General Cornwallis. Nelson's home was destroyed, leaving him bankrupt when he died.

The British seized the home of Francis Hopkinson of New Jersey, and for seven years occupied the home of William Floyd of New York.

Francis Lewis had his home and everything in it destroyed. His wife was imprisoned, and later died from the brutal treatment she had received.

After signing the Declaration, Richard Stockton, a State Supreme Court Judge, rushed back to his estate near Princeton in an effort to save his wife and children. Although he and his family found refuge with friends, a Tory betrayed them. Judge Stockton was pulled from bed in the night and was beaten by British soldiers. Then he was jailed and deliberately starved. After his release, with his home burned and all of his possessions destroyed, he and his family were forced to live off charity.

John Hart was driven from his dying wife's bedside. Their thirteen children scattered in all directions as they fled for their lives. His fields and grist mills were laid to waste. For more than a year he lived in forests and caves and returned home after the war to find his wife dead, his children gone, his properties all destroyed. He died a few weeks later of exhaustion and a broken heart without ever seeing a member of his family again.

Lewis Morris and Philip Livingston suffered fates similar to Hart's. John Hancock was known for more than his large, sweeping signature. One of the wealthiest men in New England, he stood outside Boston one terrible night of the war and said, "Burn, Boston, though it makes John Hancock a beggar, if the public good requires it." He lost most of his fortune during the war, having given over one hundred thousand dollars for the cause of freedom.

Caesar Rodney, a Delaware statesman, was gravely ill with facial cancer. Unless he returned to England for treatment, his life would end. Yet Rodney sealed his fate by signing the Declaration of Independence. He was one of several who fulfilled their pledge with their lives.

Nathan Hale also laid down his life for our nation. As a captain in the Continental Army, Hale volunteered to penetrate enemy lines to spy for the American cause. He was captured by the British. On the day of his execution by hanging in September 1776, Hale spoke these last words: "I only regret that I have but one life to lose for my country."

In all, five of the fifty-six were captured by the British and tortured. Twelve had their homes ransacked and looted, confiscated by the enemy, or burned to the ground. Seventeen lost their fortunes. Two lost their sons to the army; another had two sons captured. Nine of the fifty-six lost their lives in the war, from wounds or hardships inflicted by the enemy.[5]

A Leader in a Strange Land

Daniel was a leader. Here he is, somewhere around a junior or senior in high school. And he's a leader. He didn't have a title of leadership. He wasn't student body president or captain of the football team. He's the kid who had just transferred in from out of state. Nobody knows him. He has no connections. He has no "in" with a teacher. He doesn't even speak their language!

But Daniel was a leader.

Daniel had no title of leadership or position of leadership. But that didn't stop him from leading. Warren Bennis says that "the effective leader has to size up the situation, forge a new path to the future, and have a message and vision that have meaning to people."[6]

Daniel had sized up the situation and refused to punt on his conviction. He forged a new path to the future. And what was the upshot? He offered Ashpenaz a ten-day free trial on vegetables for his buddies and him.

He had a message and vision that had meaning. Ashpenaz, a Babylonian official, bought into Daniel's vision even though it could have cost him his life. Why did he do that?

I think it was because he trusted Daniel. Bennis makes another significant point about leadership:

What's so tricky about leading from voice [or message] and vision, rather than leading from position and perceived power? The underlying issue in leading from voice is trust; in fact, I believe that trust is the underlying issue in not only getting people on your side, but having them stay there.[7]

This is speculation on my part, but it certainly appears that Ashpenaz trusted the teenager from Judah because he backed it up. Daniel backed up his vision and his alternative plan with his life. He had obviously shown Ashpenaz that he could be trusted. He had done something to get this Bablyonian to go along with him. I think Ashpenaz had watched Daniel. I think he had watched his behavior toward his new superiors, observed his attitude toward living in a foreign culture and how he related to others. And he saw something in Daniel's life that backed up Daniel's conviction. Daniel had earned Ashpenaz's trust. Hundreds of years earlier, another young man named Joseph earned the trust of an Egyptian captain named Potiphar. And that Egyptian placed the young Hebrew in charge of everything he owned.

Daniel was in a life-threatening situation. And he wanted to live! He wanted to make a go of it in this foreign culture. He was open to all kinds of changes that God hadn't specifically forbidden. But when it came to something God *had* forbidden (eating the food from the king's table), Daniel *stood up*. But that not's all he did.

He offered up (an alternative).

Now why did he do that? He did it because he was a leader. There is a great line that comes later in the book of Daniel: "The people who know their God will display strength and take action" (Dan. 11:32). That's exactly what Daniel did when his back was up against the wall.

But Daniel made up his mind that he would not defile himself with the king's choice food or with the wine which he drank; so he sought permission from the commander of the officials that he might not defile himself.

Now God granted Daniel favor and compassion in the sight of the commander of the officials, and the commander of the officials said to Daniel, "I am afraid of my lord the king, who has appointed your food and your drink; for why should he see your faces looking more haggard than the youths who are your own age? Then you would make me forfeit my head to the king."

But Daniel said to the overseer whom the commander of the officials had appointed over Daniel, Hananiah, Mishael and Azariah, "Please test your servants for ten days, and let us be given some vegetables to eat and water to drink.

"Then let our appearance be observed in your presence, and the appearance of the youths who are eating the king's choice food; and deal with your servants according to what you see."

So he listened to them in this matter and tested them for ten days.

And at the end of ten days their appearance seemed better and they were fatter than all the youths who had been eating the king's choice food.

So the overseer continued to withhold their choice food and the wine they were to drink, and kept giving them vegetables. (Dan. 1:8–16)

Daniel didn't just give them an ultimatum. He gave them an option.

That's smart.

That's wisdom.

That's leadership.

In chapter 2 of Daniel's book, we read of another situation that occurred when their lives were on the line. "Then Daniel replied with discretion and discernment to Arioch, the captain of the king's bodyguard" (Dan. 2:14).

That's exactly what Daniel did in this situation. He knew that he couldn't eat the food that was being offered at the king's table. So he stood up and told them of his conviction.

He told them what he couldn't do . . .

But then he told them what he could do.

Too many Christians will say what they can't do. But they never say what they *can* do. They never give an option. You've met these kinds of believers. They are very quick to draw lines. They love to draw lines. They draw lines the Bible never draws. And they are willing to die for those lines. This kind of believer isn't much fun to be around. He delights in being disagreeable! And he would never consider an option to a line that he has drawn. As you might imagine, unbelievers find this person very unattractive. He leaves a bad taste in the mouths of those who don't know Christ (and of those who do!). That's because he is lacking in discretion and discernment. This type of person is hard, stubborn, and not real pleasant to be around. And there is something else about him: God doesn't use him.

Joni Eareckson Tada illustrates the difference between a Daniel with discretion and discernment and a believer with an opposite outlook:

I recall visiting a sculptor's studio. She was working on several designs, large lumps of clay in various stages of completion. Each piece sat on a turnstile, covered with damp cheesecloth, in a shaded section of her studio. The sculptor moved from one design to another, assured that each piece would remain soft, pliable, and supple until she returned.

The clay could readily harden if the humidity or temperature in her studio changed even slightly. But not so with the wax my sculptor friend used in designing pieces for reproduction. It remained soft and pliable, easy to work with. Whenever she wanted to create a work of art, she would warm the wax with a hair dryer, and it was immediately ready for work.

Hardened clay is brittle, easily damaged. If dropped, it can fracture into a thousand pieces. Dropped wax, however, only bends from the pressure of a fall. Impressionable and pliable, it can be quickly remodeled.[8]

My point is this: Daniel stood up for a conviction. He was willing to die for that conviction. He drew a line that he would not cross. On that, he was unmoving. But he wasn't so set in his ways that he couldn't propose a creative, win-win alternative to his Babylonian commander. He was pliable enough that he could recommend a solution that would be a win-win situation for everyone. That's what it means to have discretion and discernment. It means that you can lead and work with people who don't hold to the same morality that you do, not by giving up your conviction, but by showing them a better way. That's precisely what Daniel did.

Daniel wasn't antagonistic. He wasn't rude. He didn't whine or threaten. Daniel knew how to work with people.

Now, so far, here's what we've noticed about Daniel in his hostile situation:

He stood up.

He offered up (an alternative).

He backed it up (with his life).

But also notice that:

He went up (the chain of command).

Daniel didn't go *around* Ashpenaz. He went straight to the man's office and set forth his plan. Daniel was under the authority of Ashpenaz, and he determined to work within that authority structure. He didn't try to buck him, dodge him, or go over his head. He told Ashpenaz his difficulty with the food, and then he offered up an option.

The reason that he went to Ashpenaz was that he was under Ashpenaz. And Ashpenaz had his own neck on the line in this situation. If Daniel and his sidekicks were to show up at the weigh-in looking even slightly anorexic, it was all over for Ashpenaz.

How in the world did Daniel convince this Babylonian eunuch to put his own neck on the block? The answer is that God granted Daniel favor and compassion with Ashpenaz. But what form did that favor take?

Ashpenaz must have admired this young Jewish boy and his friends who were willing to stand up for their convictions. There had to be something about their willingness to put it all on the line that appealed to him.

And when Daniel approached him with the option of going vegetarian, I think there had to be a sense that Daniel was not doing this just for himself. This wasn't a self-centered act. Undoubtedly, Ashpenaz was often being approached by those under him for some favor or leniency. But this request was different. It was a matter of principle for Daniel. And Ashpenaz knew that.

The stakes couldn't have been higher—for everyone, including

Ashpenaz. But there was something about this teenager's life that must have seemed like a breath of fresh air in the stale, calculated, cover-your-trail world of Bablylonian politics. Here were four boys standing on a religious principle in a climate that was notoriously immoral.

Is it possible that Ashpenaz realized in his heart that Daniel wasn't after anything? He didn't have an agenda that would put him out in front of the other boys. Here was a young man willing to lay down his life for what he believed. And perhaps this hit a responsive chord in the heart of this Babylonian. Here was someone who actually believed in something! These Hebrew guys were willing to act on their convictions. And they didn't go around him in order to get their way.

This is all speculation, of course, but here's something that isn't. Ashpenaz knew that there was something different about these four Jewish boys. And because of this, he took a deep breath, let it out slowly . . . and granted them their ten-day request.

Now note the progression here.

Daniel stood up.

Daniel offered up (an alternative).

Daniel backed it up (with his life).

Daniel went up (the chain of command).

And as a result . . .

God backed him up.

God saw the character and the attitude of these four teenage boys as they lived under a new culture and a new regime. He saw that their hearts were fully His. And He backed them up and honored them.

As for these four young men, God gave them knowledge and skill in all literature and wisdom; and Daniel had understanding in all visions and dreams.

Now at the end of the days, when the king had said that they should be brought in, the chief of the eunuchs brought them in before Nebuchadnezzar. Then the king interviewed them, and among them all none was found like Daniel, Hananiah, Mishael, and Azariah; therefore they served before the king.

And in all matters of wisdom and understanding about which the king examined them, he found them ten times better than all the magicians and astrologers who were in all his realm. (Dan. 1:17–20 NKJV)

So . . .

How do you survive if it all comes down?

You stand up.

If need be, you offer up.

You back it up.

You go up.

And God will back you up.

But there's something else that is critical. We've alluded to it numerous times in this chapter, but we haven't focused upon it.

You team up.

Why did Daniel need a team? Why do we need a team? A team that I'm a part of has put it this way: We do together what we can't do alone.

That's teamwork.

And it's a nonnegotiable.

8

TEAMS WORK

Everybody is crazy from time to time, but it is rare that two people are crazy at the same moment.

—Michael Useem

WHEN JUDGMENT COMES, you are going to need a team.

There are two things in life you can't do by yourself. You can't get married by yourself. At least, not yet. I'm sure there is some federal judge somewhere who will rule before long that you *can* get married by yourself.

Second, you can't live the Christian life by yourself. Jesus didn't send out the disciples one by one. He sent them out two by two. Why?

Because Christianity is a team sport.

Christianity is not tennis or golf. You play those sports by yourself. Christianity is football, basketball, baseball, soccer, and hockey. You can only play those on a team.

To be without a team is a fatal error. God did not design us to live in isolation.

The story is told of a reclusive woman who lived by herself. Not only did she live by herself, she stayed to herself. She only went out to the store when she absolutely had to. If anyone greeted her, she would not respond. She would not engage anyone in conversation. Not the grocer, the postman, the pharmacist, nor anyone at the doctor's office. She didn't go to church, so she had no friends there. She never talked with her neighbors.

One evening, the mortuary called the newspaper to tell them that the woman had died and that they needed to write an obituary for her. The reporter for the paper had no idea what to write. No one knew anything about her. She had no family and no friends. No one in the town knew anything about her background or her life because she always stayed to herself. He was absolutely stumped as to what he should say.

His deadline was 5:00 P.M. the next afternoon. After talking to everyone he could think of who might give him information, he came up empty.

Finally he sat down at the typewriter and pecked out these words:

> Here lie the bones of Nancy Jones
> For her life held no terrors.
> She lived an old maid. She died an old maid.
> No hits, no runs, no errors.

There is nothing wrong with being single and not dating. But there is everything wrong with being a recluse and not having any contact with people. If you're not on a team, you're not in the game. The Christian life is a team sport. And the need for a team is felt most acutely in times of crisis. Judgment is one of those times.

Daniel's Team

Daniel watched the judgment of God slam into his nation with devastating force. After centuries of trying to get Judah's attention, God had to send the curses of Deuteronomy 28 upon them. They were invaded by Nebuchadnezzar in A.D. 605, the first of three sieges by this Babylonian king. In this first visitation of Nebuchadnezzar, he took some of the choice young men back to Babylon to reprogram them.

Daniel was one of those. But he wasn't alone. He had a team. We know his teammates better by their Babylonian names Shadrach, Meschach, and Abed-nego. But their Jewish names were Hananiah, Mishael, and Azariah. These teenage boys saw their world turn completely upside down. As we saw in the last chapter, they were carried off to Babylon, never to see Jerusalem again.

They were thrown into a new culture and forced to change everything in their lives. They changed names, languages, colleges, and friends. But even under tremendous pressure and threat of death, they refused to change gods. How did they survive in such circumstances?

I would submit to you that they relied on the team.

They didn't try to pull it off by themselves. They knew that if they were to survive in this new nation with its pagan laws and customs, they would need to stick together. And that's precisely what they did.

As you read through the book of Daniel, it is very apparent that these four young men were committed to one another. These guys were as close as David and Jonathan. They were going to look out for each other.

Let's observe the team by taking a quick survey through Daniel:

● *They stood up as a team.*

We looked at these verses in the last chapter, but let's observe them from the "team" perspective. Note that Daniel is the obvious leader of the team. He is the spokesman. But throughout this passage it is apparent that although Daniel is the up-front guy, he is conveying the conviction of the team. The give-and-take between singular and plural pronouns brings this home:

But Daniel made up his mind that he would not defile himself with the king's choice food or with the wine which he drank; so he sought permission from the commander of the officials that he might not defile himself. Now God granted Daniel favor and compassion in the sight of the commander of the officials, and the commander of the officials said to Daniel, "I am afraid of my lord the king, who has appointed your food and your drink; for why should he see your faces looking more haggard than the youths who are your own age? Then you would make me forfeit my head to the king."

But Daniel said to the overseer whom the commander of the officials had appointed over Daniel, Hananiah, Mishael and Azariah, "Please test your servants for ten days, and let us be given some vegetables to eat and water to drink.

"Then let *our* appearance be observed in your presence, and the appearance of the youths who are eating the king's choice food; and deal with your servants according to what you see."

So he listened to them in this matter and tested them for ten days. (Dan. 1:8–14)

These four young men operated as one. Daniel was the quarter-back, but when he spoke, he spoke for all of them. It is important to understand that their hearts were one. They weren't divided over this issue. They were of one mind that they wouldn't eat the food.

They made this decision even though they knew very well their lives were on the line. And when an issue becomes a literal life-or-death issue, you'd better make sure you know who your wingmen are. You'd better have the right teammates.

Sadhu Sundar Singh and a companion were traveling through a high pass in the Himalayan mountains when they came across a body lying in the snow. They checked for vital signs and discovered the man still alive, but barely so. Sundar Singh prepared to stop and help this unfortunate traveler, but his companion objected, saying, "We shall lose our lives if we burden ourselves with him." Sundar Singh, however, could not think of leaving the man to die in the snow without an attempted rescue on his part. His companion quickly bade him farewell and walked on.

Sundar Singh lifted the poor traveler onto his back. With great exertion on his part—made even greater by the high altitude and snowy conditions—he carried the man onward. As he walked, the heat cast off his body began to warm the frozen man. He revived, and soon both were walking together side by side, each holding the other up, and in turn each giving body heat to the other. Before long they came upon yet another traveler's body lying in the snow. Upon closer inspection they discovered him to be dead, frozen by the snow.

It was Sundar Singh's original traveling companion.

Those four teenagers had the same heart. They weren't going to cut and run the first time they encountered a problem. They had the same values and the same convictions. And that's why they stood tall in a day of judgment.

• *They were rewarded as a team.*

And at the end of ten days their appearance seemed better and they were fatter than all the youths who had been eating the king's choice food.

So the overseer continued to withhold their choice food and the wine they were to drink, and kept giving them vegetables.

And as for these four youths, God gave them knowledge and intelligence in every branch of literature and wisdom; Daniel even understood all kinds of visions and dreams.

Then at the end of the days which the king had specified for presenting them, the commander of the officials presented them before Nebuchadnezzar.

And the king talked with them, and out of them all not one was found like Daniel, Hananiah, Mishael and Azariah; so they entered the king's personal service.

And as for every matter of wisdom and understanding about which the king consulted them, he found them ten times better than all the magicians and conjurers who were in all his realm. (Dan. 1:15–20)

They stood as a team, and God rewarded them as a team. This is why it is so important to know the hearts of those on your team. These young men were completely sold out. There were willing to put it all on the line. There wasn't a weak link in the bunch. And as a result, they enjoyed the favor and blessing of God together.

If you team up with someone who is weak in conviction and values, inevitably that is going to bring you down.

The character issue relates not only to individuals, it relates to a team. One bad apple can affect the entire team. You can't afford to have sin in the camp.

When Joshua led the children of Israel against the city of Jericho, God made it very clear that the silver and gold of the city were to go into the treasury of the Lord (Josh. 6:18–7:26). But a man named Achan took some silver and gold and hid it. After defeating Jericho, Joshua led Israel against the city of Ai. Of course, they expected that God would give them victory. But they were defeated, and thirty-six brave men were killed. Joshua couldn't understand why God had let them down. Then the Lord revealed that one man had violated God's word. And it had cost Israel thirty-six men. The nation of Israel paid for the sin of Achan, because he violated the ban that God had set on the spoils of Jericho. And he cost them the reward that God wanted to give to them.

We never sin alone. Our sin always affects others. When you select a team, look out for the compromisers. Avoid the Achan's like the plague. And ask God to give you a Daniel, Shadrach, Meshach, and Abed-nego.

• They prayed as a team.

In chapter 2, a new situation develops with Nebuchadnezzar. The king had a dream that deeply troubled him. It was so problematic he couldn't sleep.

Then Nebuchadnezzar did something very unusual. He assembled all of his magicians, psychics, and soothsayers, and asked them to tell him the dream. Usually the king would tell them about the dream, and then they would interpret for him. But not this time.

He decided to put the ball in their court. In other words, "If you guys are so smart, tell me what my dream was!" This is all described in Daniel 2:1–3. In the next verses, they respond to the king.

Then the Chaldeans spoke to the king in Aramaic: "O king, live forever! Tell the dream to your servants, and we will declare the interpretation."

The king answered and said to the Chaldeans, "The command from me is firm: if you do not make known to me the dream and its interpretation, you will be torn limb from limb, and your houses will be made a rubbish heap.

"But if you declare the dream and its interpretation, you will receive from me gifts and a reward and great honor; therefore declare to me the dream and its interpretation."

They answered a second time and said, "Let the king tell the dream to his servants, and we will declare the interpretation."

The king answered and said, "I know for certain that you are bargaining for time, inasmuch as you have seen that the command from me is firm, that if you do not make the dream known to me, there is only one decree for you. For you have agreed together to speak lying and corrupt words before me until the situation is changed; therefore tell me the dream, that I may know that you can declare to me its interpretation."

The Chaldeans answered the king and said, "There is not a man on earth who could declare the matter for the king, inasmuch as no great king or ruler has ever asked anything like this of any magician, conjurer or Chaldean.

"Moreover, the thing which the king demands is difficult, and there is no one else who could declare it to the king except gods, whose dwelling place is not with mortal flesh."

Because of this the king became indignant and very furious, and gave orders to destroy all the wise men of Babylon.

So the decree went forth that the wise men should be slain; and they looked for Daniel and his friends to kill them. (vv. 4–13)

Daniel and his three amigos were obviously not in on this meeting. But they quickly found out about it!

Then Daniel replied with discretion and discernment to Arioch, the captain of the king's bodyguard, who had gone forth to slay the wise men of Babylon; he answered and said to Arioch, the king's commander, "For what reason is the decree from the king so urgent?" Then Arioch informed Daniel about the matter.

So Daniel went in and requested of the king that he would give him time, in order that he might declare the interpretation to the king. (Dan. 2:14–16)

It tells us something about the influence of Daniel that he was able to get an audience with the king. This was not an easy thing to do. But God had given Daniel favor with the king. And then Daniel did something that took a lot of courage. He asked for more time. The king had already said he wouldn't give more time, but when the request came from Daniel, he consented. Now, watch how Daniel turns to his team.

> Then Daniel went to his house and informed his friends, Hananiah, Mishael and Azariah, about the matter, in order that they might request compassion from the God of heaven concerning this mystery, so that Daniel and his friends might not be destroyed with the rest of the wise men of Babylon. (Dan. 2:17–18)

These young men immediately began to pray. Let me ask you a question. Everyone is part of some kind of team. When a crisis hits your life, you turn to a few people. Are those people on your team *praying* people? Do they know the Lord? Do they seek Him? If not, you had better get a new team.

I recently heard that when Joni Eareckson Tada travels into a foreign country for ministry, she will often bring a team of seasoned prayer warriors with her. That's all these folks do. Before every event, before every leg of the journey, this tried-and-true prayer team hit their knees and cry out to God for His grace and favor. Joni understands that Christianity is a team sport.

Daniel and his friends quickly went before the Lord. They asked Him to do the impossible! They asked Him to tell them the dream. And they didn't have much time. Their situation brings to mind Hebrews 4:16: "Let us therefore draw near with confidence to the throne of grace, that we may receive mercy and may find grace to help in time of need." John Piper says that "the Greek original behind the phrase 'grace to help in time of need,' would be translated literally, 'grace for a well-timed help.'"[1]

That is precisely what Daniel and the boys needed. They needed a "well-timed help" because they were just about out of time. So "Team Judah" went to its knees.

> Then the mystery was revealed to Daniel in a night vision. Then
> Daniel blessed the God of heaven;
> Daniel answered and said,
> "Let the name of God be blessed forever and ever,
> For wisdom and power belong to Him.
> And it is He who changes the times and the epochs;
> He removes kings and establishes kings;
> He gives wisdom to wise men,
> And knowledge to men of understanding.
> It is He who reveals the profound and hidden things;
> He knows what is in the darkness,
> And the light dwells with Him.
> To Thee, O God of my fathers, I give thanks and praise,
> For Thou hast given me wisdom and power;
> Even now Thou hast made known to *me* what we requested of Thee,
> For Thou hast made known to *us* the king's matter."
> (Dan. 2:19–23, emphasis mine)

• *God answered them as a team.*

They went to their knees as a team, and they got an answer as a team. Daniel indicates that God made it known to him what they requested. And in the next line, he says that God had made known to *them* the matter. Once again, he goes back and forth between the singular and the plural. Apparently, the Lord made the dream known to Daniel. Daniel was part of the team. Thus, God made it known to all of them.

That's how close teams think.

When Daniel received the interpretation, he didn't run around, strutting and pointing to himself. Team members don't draw attention to themselves. Daniel didn't even give credit to the team. He gave credit to the Lord.

Do you have anyone who will go to the mat with you in prayer? Do you have a team willing to pray with you and for you when you are in the middle of crunch time? To know that a team is praying for you gives great hope and motivation.

People are motivated by different things. One of the most grueling things a human can do is to try to break the world record for the one-mile run. The first to break four minutes in the mile was Roger Bannister. He was enabled to achieve such a great accomplishment by a particular motivation. Following is a list of men who broke the world record in the mile. Note how each of them was motivated differently from others who were seeking the same goal:

Roger Bannister (1954, 3:59.4): "Running presents a perfect test of judgment, speed, and stamina."

John Landy (1954, 3:58): "One's effort could be pinned down and quantified precisely."

Derek Ibbotsond (1957, 3:57): "I ran to prove to my father that I was better than my brother."

Herb Elliot (1958, 3:54.5): "I ran at first to remorselessly beat everyone I possibly could."

Peter Snell (1964, 3:54.1): "I ran for recognition."

Michel Jazy (1965, 3:53): "I ran so I would not have to fight the war in Algeria."

Jim Ryun (1965, 3:51): "I ran to get a letter jacket and a girl-friend."

Sebastian Coe (1981, 3:47): "I ran because I was meant to run."

Noureddine Morceli (1993, 3:44): "I run to be known as the greatest runner . . . of all time."

Robert Murray McCheyne was very clear about what moti-vated him:

> "If I could hear Christ praying for me in the next room, I would not fear a million enemies. Yet distance makes no difference. He *is* praying for me."

Maybe you are at a point in your life where you are isolated and alone. You're thinking to yourself that you don't have a team and that no one is praying for you. Yet that isn't so. Even if you can't find a team, you're on His team. The Lord Jesus Christ is praying for you! "Hence, also, He is able to save forever those who draw near to God through Him, since He always lives to make interces-sion for them" (Heb. 7:25).

How to Find a Team

Reading about the teamwork of Daniel and his three sidekicks is very exciting. Wouldn't it be great to have a team like that? If times get hard, and if judgment is coming on this nation, you and I are going to need a team as Daniel needed a team.

The Mysterious Island, a novel by Jules Verne, is the story of five men who escape a Civil War prison camp by hijacking a hot-air balloon. Very quickly, they realize the wind is carrying them out over the ocean. As the hours pass, they see the horizon receding and realize they are also losing altitude. Since they have no way to heat the air in the balloon, they begin to throw some of the excess weight overboard. Shoes, coats, and weapons are reluctantly discarded, yet they rejoice that the balloon begins to rise.

Soon, however, they draw dangerously close to the waves again and begin to toss their food overboard. Better to be aloft and hungry! Yet a third time the balloon begins to descend, and this time one of the men suggests they tie together the ropes that connect the balloon to the basket in which they are riding, and then sit on the ropes and cut away the heavy basket. The very floor they had been standing on falls away, and the balloon rises once again.

Suddenly, they spot land. With not a minute to spare, they jump into the water and swim to an island. Their lives are spared, not because of any great heroics, but because they had learned what they could live without.[2]

And what they couldn't live without was one another.

They survived because they were a team. If hard times are coming (and they are) then you are going to need to be a part of something bigger than yourself.

I just got off the phone with a friend who is being greatly used of the Lord. Without going into the details, I can tell you this. He is influencing a large number of people for Christ. There are those who are not pleased with that fact. And as a result, he is experiencing tremendous public criticism and character assassination. What makes this really tough is that the criticism is coming from other Christians.

Fortunately this man has a team. He considers me part of his prayer team and dialed my number when he was feeling isolated and under the gun. I know very well that he would do the same thing for me. Everyone needs a team. Especially when times get tough.

Here's a game plan for putting together a team for the tough times that are coming:

- You need your spouse on your team.

- You need extended family on your team.

- You need a close friend on your team.

- You need a church on your team.

- You need neighbors on your team.

Now let's quickly point out that you may not have all of these folks on your team. You may not have a spouse; you may be single. Or you may not be near any extended family. Not everyone is going to have the ideal situation. But this will help you get started.

One other thing. If you don't have a team, you will need to take the initiative. You can't wait for relationships to come knocking on your front door. You have to be out there, you have to be circulating, you have to be with people in order for teamwork to occur. Now let's look at these aspects of team-building individually. And remember, we are talking about a context like Daniel's, where life has fallen apart. If judgment occurs and life is hard and difficult, you are going to need a team to get you through just as Daniel did.

• *You need your spouse on your team.*

Ulysses Grant was the greatest general that the North had during the Civil War. Abraham Lincoln's greatest problem was a lack of leadership among his generals. But when he moved Grant up to lead, things began to happen. Grant began to win! But Grant had a reputation as a drunk. Yet Lincoln had such appreciation for

Grant, he said, "I don't know what he's drinking, but I need to send a case of it to my other generals." In actuality, Grant was not a drunk. He simply missed his wife. Geoffrey Perret fills us in on the details:

> It's ironic, but the most famous drunk in American history was not a heavy drinker. The trouble with Grant was that he could get drunk on two drinks. Not only that, he would start walking into the furniture and need the wall for support. It was obvious when Grant had been drinking . . . There was only one reason why Grant drank and that was he was deeply and passionately in love with his wife.
>
> Grant's marriage was not a limited partnership. It was a romance from beginning to end. When he was away from Julia for very long, he felt desperately lonely. He missed her tremendously. He would start drinking. It's also true during the Civil War, after some big battle, Grant would have a couple of drinks. This was more or less a release of tension. But while he was preparing for battle, while battle was in progress, he never touched the stuff.
>
> The presence of a bottle in Grant's tent invariably indicated the absence of Julia. When the war ended and he was able to spend all of his time with his wife, he hardly ever touched anything except maybe to sip a glass of champagne at a state banquet in the White House.[3]

Grant was in the midst of hard times. Life as he knew it and enjoyed it had been interrupted. And he needed his wife. Without her, he was lonely and incomplete. He missed her company and their conversation.

When hardship comes, you and your spouse must work as a

team. So often we allow ourselves to become divided by small and insignificant things. When life gets hard, you just can't afford that. You are going to have to function as a team. What if the economy goes down and your husband loses his job? That's not a time to be divided! That's when you must pull together!

Every couple has their disagreements. You and your spouse may have different personalities, different temperaments, and different approaches to finances. So often it's the differences that drive us crazy. But it's those very same differences that make us a good team. Teams are made up of people who play different positions. What are your strengths? What are your weaknesses? How about your spouse? What are his or her strengths and weaknesses?

When you actually put this down on paper, it can be a real revelation. The strengths and weaknesses of each spouse tend to balance out. In other words, you are stronger together than you are apart . . . just as the Lord intended it to be.

That's why you need each other.

A wife may have tremendous discernment but just average people skills. Yet she may be married to a man who is weak on the discernment side, but incredible with people. Now that's a team. That's life. Together you are more effective than you are apart!

Instead of letting the differences drive you crazy, thank God for them. Those differences, when you can learn to appreciate them, are a gift that He has given to you to make the two of you stronger.

There are certain things you can say that will build your relationship. There are certain things you can say that won't build it at all. Steve Stephens offers "27 Things Not to Say to Your Spouse."[4]

1. "I told you so."

2. "You're just like your mother [or father]."

3. "You're always in a bad mood."

4. "You just don't think."

5. "It's your fault."

6. "What's wrong with you?"

7. "All you ever do is complain."

8. "I can't do anything to please you."

9. "You get what you deserve."

10. "Why don't you ever listen to me?"

11. "Can't you be more responsible?"

12. "What were you thinking?"

13. "You're impossible!"

14. "I don't know why I put up with you."

15. "I can talk to you until I'm blue in the face, and it doesn't do any good."

16. "I can do whatever I like."

17. "If you don't like it, you can just leave."

18. "Can't you do anything right?"

19. "That was stupid."

20. "All you ever do is think of yourself."

21. "If you really loved me, you'd do this."

22. "You're such a baby."

23. "Turnabout's fair play."

24. "You deserve a dose of your own medicine."

25. "What's your problem?"

26. "I can never understand you."

27. "Do you always have to be right?"

In contrast, here are 37 things that you *can* say to your spouse.

1. "Good job!"

2. "You are wonderful!"

3. "That was really great!"

4. "You look gorgeous [or handsome] today!"

5. "I don't feel complete without you."

6. "I appreciate all the things you've done for me all these years."

7. "You come first in my life [on earth], before kids, career, friends, anything."

8. "I'm glad I married you."

9. "You're the best friend I have."

10. "If I had to do it all over again, I would marry you."

11. "I wanted you today."

12. "I missed you today."

13. "I couldn't get you out of my mind today."

14. "It's nice to wake up next to you."

15. "I will always love you."

16. "I love to see your eyes sparkle when you smile."

17. "As always, you look good today."

18. "I trust you."

19. "I can always count on you."

20. "You make me feel good."

21. "I'm so proud to be married to you."

22. "I'm sorry."

23. "I was wrong."

24. "What would you like?"

25. "What's on your mind?"

26. "Let me just listen."

27. "You are so special."

28. "I can't imagine life without you."

29. "I wish I were a better partner."

30. "What can I do to help?"

31. "Pray for me."

32. "I'm praying for you today."

33. "I prize every moment we spend together."

34. "Thank you for loving me."

35. "Thank you for accepting me."

36. "Thank you for being my partner."

37. "You make every day brighter."

Helen Douglas said it best: "When a marriage works, nothing on earth can take its place."

• *You need extended family on your team.*

Not everyone has this. But if you do, you are very fortunate. This past Christmas, we had twenty-six family members at our house! The bedrooms were full, and the kids were sleeping on the floor, but we had a blast. For all I know, some of them were sleeping in the car.

But what a team. And in times of crisis, we pull together. In the last year, some of those twenty-six had been in deep crisis and hardship. One of them had gone through a divorce. Another had been laid off and couldn't find work for ten months. Another person was struggling with depression. Now those twenty-six live in four different states. We don't all live in the same neighborhood. But when someone in California is hurting, they usually get together with the other family members in California. And the rest of us in Arizona, Colorado, and Texas get on the phone. You can still have a team even if you are separated by hundreds of miles.

It's hard when your extended family doesn't know the Lord. But they are still family. They may not be able to stand with you spiritually because they are spiritually blind. But they still love you, and you love them. And as you keep those communications line open, they will see the reality of Christ in your life. If life gets hard as the result of judgment, they are going to need a connection with someone who can tell them about Christ. So keep the communication lines flowing as best you can. I know that it's hard because they don't know the Lord. But when they realize their need for Him, they will turn to you. That's worth keeping as close as possible to them.

• *You need a close friend on your team.*

When times are hard and difficult, and life falls apart, you need someone that you can share your heart with. Christianity is a team sport, remember?

Friends can make you or break you.

In Exodus 17, we read the account of Israel being attacked by the Amalekites. Perhaps you remember the story. As long as Moses held his hand up, Israel would prevail. When he let his hand down, the Amalekites would get the advantage. Moses held in his hands the rod of God. As the Israelites were fighting down in the valley, they would steal a glimpse of Moses up on the hill, holding the rod. That rod was like a banner to those fighting men. One of the names of God is "Jehovah-Nissi," which means "the Lord is my banner." To see Moses holding up the rod of God reminded them that the Lord was with them.

But the battle raged on for hours. Moses could not keep his hands in the air that long. So some friends came along and gave him some assistance. Aaron and Hur got a good-size rock and told Moses to have a seat. Then they each took an arm and supported it.

That's a remarkable picture of friendship.

Moses was encouraging the men in the valley that God is their friend and deliverer. But in order for Moses to encourage his friends in the valley, he needed some friends to encourage him.

Just like Daniel, Shadrach, Meshach, and Abed-nego.

David and Jonathan.

Paul and Silas.

Need I go on?

If they needed a friend, you need a friend. One you can trust. One you can walk through life with. One you can count on. Have you got one? If not, ask God for one. There is nothing more valuable than one close friend.

• *You need a church on your team.*

Let me be more specific. You need a church that takes the Bible seriously. A church that believes in the authority, inspiration, and inerrancy of the Bible. If they take the Bible seriously, they take Jesus Christ seriously. This is important because when judgment comes you're going to need a church—not a country club.

There are two responsibilities of a church: birth and growth.

A church is there to lead people to Christ.

Billy Graham tells of arriving in a small town to preach. When he got into town, he asked a young boy for directions to the post office, so he could put a letter in the mail. After getting directions from the boy, he invited him to the service that evening. "I'm going to tell people how to get to heaven." The boy replied, "I don't think I'll be there, mister. You don't even know how to get to the post office." Make sure that your church lets people know that heaven is a free gift. That's birth.

But churches are also responsible for *growing* those new babes in Christ. That's discipleship. Young and old Christians need a steady diet of biblical teaching so that they can grow. And then they need to be trained to use their spiritual gifts so that they don't stagnate.

Historically, when hard times come there is no more important place to be than with other believers.

Churches come in different sizes and denominations. But there are some essentials that must be there. Here is the irreducible minimum:

- They need to believe in one God, existing in three persons: the Father, the Son, and the Holy Spirit.

- They need to believe in the absolute authority, inspiration, and inerrancy of the Bible.

- They need to believe that Jesus was born of a virgin, that He lived a sinless life, that He went to the cross to shed His blood for the atonement of sin, that He was buried, and that on the third day, He literally, historically, and physically rose from the dead.

- They need to believe that Jesus ascended to the Father, where He sits at the right hand, making intercession for believers.

- They need to believe that "by grace you have been saved through faith; and that not of yourselves, it is the gift of God; not as a result of works, that no one should boast" (Eph. 2:8–9).

- They need to believe in the second coming of Jesus Christ to the earth.

You can't live the Christian life by yourself. And you don't want to try. Churches come in different flavors. They have different kinds of music, different styles of preaching, and different affiliations. But what they have in common is submission and love to Christ. When judgment comes, those are the people who will experience God's favor. And you want to be right smack in the middle of it.

• *You need some neighbors on your team.*

If you are like most Americans, you don't even know the people who live on either side of you. You might know their names, but that's it.

Let me encourage you to consider taking a bold step. Invite them over for dinner. Throw some hamburgers on the grill. No big deal. It doesn't have to be a state dinner with your best china and silver. Paper plates will do. All you want to do is to get acquainted. Get to know them. Start a relationship.

Don't feel that you have to hard-sell the gospel. Let them know that you are normal. Let them know that you are interested in them. Just that, alone, will give them a hint that something is different in your home.

Maybe this is an idea that makes you a little nervous. Maybe evangelism isn't your strong suit. It doesn't have to be. You don't need to give an altar call at the end of dinner. You don't even need to steer the conversation to spiritual issues.

Just be a friend. Be a good neighbor. And let the Holy Spirit take it from there. Who knows what the Lord might do in His time?

It doesn't take much to get a neighbor on your team. A casual meal and a few laughs over ice cream. That may be all it takes to arouse their interest in the One who died to save them from judgment.

Wouldn't it be great to see them join His team?

9

CONVICTION UNDER FIRE

God is preparing his heroes; and when the opportunity comes, he can fit them into their places in a moment, and the world will wonder where they came from.

—A. B. Simpson

FOR WAGNER DODGE the hour struck on August 5, 1949. And he wasn't expecting it. He and his crew jumped into a plane to fight a fire at Mann Gulch in central Montana. It was just another day for Dodge and his smoke jumpers. They could have used a few more hours of rest, but when the mountains are bone dry there is no time to rest.

From the air it looked like a pretty normal operation. They jumped and landed without incident. They gathered up their chutes and headed single file down the gorge toward the Missouri River to take on the fire. Dodge left the men in the middle of the gorge to scout what was ahead. As he got within one hundred feet of the fire, he made three discoveries that would change his life forever.

First, he realized that the fire was much worse than the view from overhead had led him to believe. The wind was coming over the ridge and whipping this fire a lot faster than he had realized. Second, the swirling winds were blowing the fire above the gulch, up to the ridge. In other words, their escape route was cut off. Third, as he directed his men to retreat, he realized that this gulch was in a transitional zone.

A forest fire rarely moves at more than four or five miles an hour, an advance that smoke jumpers can always outrun. But Mann Gulch was part of a transitional zone—an area where mountains yield to plains, and forest timber to prairie grass—and as the men fled from the fire, the forest gave way to shoulder-high grass—dense, dry, and ready to explode.

The Plains Indians feared a prairie grass fire almost as much as anything. The knew that the worst could not be outrun, and now Dodge knew it too. His mind in steely control, Dodge estimated that as fast as he and his men could move up what was now becoming a grassy slope, the towering wall of fire would move faster. Within a minute or two, Dodge estimated, perhaps sooner, he and his men would be overtaken by flames.

The roar was deafening. Sap in scattered trees was superheating and exploding. Smoke, embers, and ashes swirled in all directions. The apparent options offered Dodge no escape: stand and be fatally burned; turn and be fatally burned; run and be fatally burned.[1]

There was no escape. Dodge and his fifteen men were trapped. Their options were closed. They had about sixty seconds to live before the fire swept over them. Suddenly Dodge stopped. He took out a match, lit it, and threw it into the shoulder-high grass in front of him. His men, watching from behind, thought he had lost his mind. There was no time to light a backfire. But Dodge wasn't lighting a backfire. He was lighting a fire. In an instant, the grass was ablaze in a widening circle.

> As the ring of his new fire spread, it cleared a small area of all flammable substances. It was not much of a safety zone, but it would have to do. He jumped over the blazing ring, moved to its smoldering center, wrapped a wet cloth around his face, pressed himself close to the ground, and waited. As he had anticipated, the surging fire wall rounded both sides of his small circle, leapt over the top, but found nothing to ignite where he lay motionless. Within moments the front passed, racing up the ridge and leaving him unscathed in his tiny asylum. He stood, brushed off the ash, and found he was no worse for wear. He had literally burned a hole in the raging fire.[2]

Two of his men saw Dodge motion with his hand for them to join him. But they ran around his fire, found an old rock slide that was relatively free from vegetation, and burrowed into the rocks.

The thirteen other men saw what Dodge had done, and decided they would be better off making a run for it. None of them made it.

Dodge survived the fire by going against human instinct. Faced with the threat of fire, he lit a fire and jumped into it. Because he was willing to step into the fire, his life was saved.

Sort of like Shadrach, Meshach, and Abed-nego.

Is There Any Good News?

It's not much fun to read a book about coming judgment. But I will assure you that it's even less fun to write it. As you read the prophets in the Old Testament, they did not fail to give hope. They reminded the people that if they would turn back to the Lord, they would see His goodness and mercy. There is always hope for the believer who is seeking first the kingdom of God.

But here's the flip side of this. If you are seeking first the kingdom of God in a culture that is opposed to God, you are going to be persecuted. There is no question about that. And to think that we will not face persecution is to deny reality. It may not be pleasant to hear, but it is the truth.

In Ezekiel 33 we read these words:

And the word of the LORD came to me saying, "Son of man, speak to the sons of your people, and say to them, 'If I bring a sword upon a land, and the people of the land take one man from among them and make him their watchman; and he sees the sword coming upon the land, and he blows on the trumpet and warns the people, then he who hears the sound of the trumpet and does not take warning, and a sword comes and takes him away, his blood will be on his own head.

'He heard the sound of the trumpet, but did not take warning; his blood will be on himself. But had he taken warning, he would have delivered his life. But if the watchman sees the sword coming and does not blow the trumpet, and the people are not warned, and a sword comes and takes a person from them, he is taken away in his iniquity; but his blood I will require from the watchman's hand.'" (vv. 1–6)

Persecution is coming.

That's not the greatest news that you've ever heard. But not to alert you to it would be sin. It really shouldn't come as a surprise.

The curtain of persecution has opened and the first act has already begun.

Last night in Fort Worth, Texas, a gunman walked into Wedgwood Baptist Church and opened fire on a group of high school students who were celebrating "See You at the Pole." As you probably know, this is an annual event in which students around the country meet before school around the flagpole for student-led prayer.

Yesterday morning I saw my friend Billy Beacham on the local television news. Billy was telling a reporter that in the midst of a nation that is collapsing under the weight of its own immorality, there is a remarkable movement taking place among high school students. There are so many kids who want to make their faith known through "See You at the Pole" that Billy's office has been getting more than one thousand calls a day from people asking for information.

Billy mentioned the profound effect that the shootings at Columbine High School have had on Christian students from around the country. But this was not the first occurrence of Christian students being shot because of their faith. The school shootings in Paducah, Kentucky, were the first example. The young man in this instance didn't open fire on everyone. He waited for the members of an early morning Bible study to walk down the hallway. He didn't shoot at everyone. He shot at Christians.

Billy was explaining to the television audience that these tragic situations have ignited a flame of spiritual renewal among teenagers across America.

Little did Billy know that just twelve hours later, a few miles away from where he was standing, seven young people and youth leaders would be added to that list of martyrs.

In Paducah, Columbine, and Fort Worth, Christians were singled out because of their faith. That is persecution. It is here. And we must understand how to conduct ourselves when persecution confronts us. There is no better place to go than to the example of three Jewish teenagers who were put to the test in ancient Babylon.

Life was actually going pretty well for them. They had recently been promoted and were enjoying a fairly high quality of life. But suddenly that all changed. Things began to heat up very quickly. And, like Warner Dodge, they concluded that their only option was to get into the fire:

> Nebuchadnezzar the king made an image of gold, the height of which was sixty cubits and and its width six cubits; he set it up on the plain of Dura in the province of Babylon.

> Then Nebuchadnezzar the king sent word to assemble the satraps, the prefects and the governors, the counselors, the treasurers, the judges, the magistrates and all the rulers of the provinces to come to the dedication of the image that Nebuchadnezzar the king had set up.

> Then the satraps, the prefects and the governors, the counselors, the treasurers, the judges, the magistrates and all the rulers of the provinces were assembled for the dedication of the image that Nebuchadnezzar the king had set up; and they stood before the image that Nebuchadnezzar had set up.

> Then the herald loudly proclaimed: "To you the command is given, O peoples, nations and men of every language, that at the moment

you hear the sound of the horn, flute, lyre, trigon, psaltery, bagpipe, and all kinds of music, you are to fall down and worship the golden image that Nebuchadnezzar the king has set up.

"But whoever does not fall down and worship shall immediately be cast into the midst of a furnace of blazing fire."

Therefore at that time, when all the peoples heard the sound of the horn, flute, lyre, trigon, psaltery, bagpipe, and all kinds of music, all the peoples, nations and men of every language fell down and worshiped the golden image that Nebuchadnezzar the king had set up. (Dan. 3:1–7)

The setting of this image probably relates back to chapter 2. In chapter 2, you remember, Nebuchadnezzar had a dream that Daniel interpreted. But before Daniel interpreted the dream, Daniel told him what his dream was. Without going into detail here about the significance of the interpretation, Daniel told him that he saw a great statue. And then in verses 36–38, Daniel tells him that the head of gold on the statue represents Nebuchadnezzar. It is quite possible that this statue of the king's dream gave him the idea of erecting a great statue. This statue was ninety feet high (sixty cubits). This would have been a remarkable sight. It made a very strong first impression. And Nebuchadnezzar planned on taking advantage of this.

The text indicates that Nebuchadnezzar brought all of the various officials from his widespread kingdom. Apparently, he wanted to use this event to unite his kingdom and establish that the various officials were in submission to him. But when he demanded themnot only to bow down, but also to worship, then he brought in the religious element. It's as though he was establishing a new state religion under this massive idol.

And he commanded everyone to bow down and worship. Whoever refused to bow down and worship was invited to step into the fire. So everyone bowed down and worshiped. Except for those who loved the Lord their God with all their heart, all their soul, and all their might.

> For this reason at that time certain Chaldeans came forward and brought charges against the Jews. They responded and said to Nebuchadnezzar the king: "O king, live forever! You yourself, O king, have made a decree that every man who hears the sound of the horn, flute, lyre, trigon, psaltery, and bagpipe, and all kinds of music, is to fall down and worship the golden image.

> "But whoever does not fall down and worship shall be cast into the midst of a furnace of blazing fire. There are certain Jews whom you have appointed over the administration of the province of Babylon, namely Shadrach, Meshach and Abednego. These men, O king, have disregarded you; they do not serve your gods or worship the golden image which you have set up." (Dan. 3:8–12)

One of the great heroes of the Civil War was Joshua Lawrence Chamberlain. It was Chamberlain who said, "We know not the future, and cannot plan for it much. But we can . . . determine and know what manner of men we will be whenever and wherever the hour strikes."

Out there on the plain of Dura, the hour struck for Shadrach, Meshach, and Abed-nego. No indication is given that the gathered officials knew that they were to bow down before the announcement was made. There is no indication they were told weeks or months prior to this great assembly that they were to worship. The order to worship was simply announced.

I'm sure that some of the audience was surprised. I'm sure that these three young Jewish men were surprised. But there was no questioning their response. They had already determined long ago their response in such an hour. They refused to bow.

Undoubtedly there was some jealousy behind the accusation of the Chaldeans. Because Daniel had interpreted the king's dream in chapter 2, Daniel was made ruler "over the whole province of Babylon and chief prefect over all the wise men of Babylon" (2:48). This meant that Daniel was the Chaldeans' boss. Then Daniel had received permission to promote Shadrach, Meshach, and Abed-nego "over the administration of the province of Babylon, while Daniel was at the king's court" (2:49).

Jewish exiles were not usually put into the corridors of power. At least, not at that level. And there had to be some resentment. So here was the perfect opportunity to put these Jewish irritants in their rightful place. They suggested to the king that these men were traitors to him, his authority, and his new god.

Then Nebuchadnezzar in rage and anger gave orders to bring Shadrach, Meshach and Abed-nego; then these men were brought before the king. Nebuchadnezzar responded and said to them, "Is it true, Shadrach, Meshach and Abed-nego, that you do not serve my gods or worship the golden image that I have set up?

"Now if you are ready, at the moment you hear the sound of the horn, flute, lyre, trigon, psaltery, and bagpipe, and all kinds of music, to fall down and worship the image that I have made, very well. But if you will not worship, you will immediately be cast into the midst of a furnace of blazing fire; and what god is there who can deliver you out of my hands?"

Shadrach, Meshach and Abed-nego anwered and said to the king, "O Nebuchadnezzar, we do not need to give you an answer concerning this. If it be so, our God whom we serve is able to deliver us from the furnace of blazing fire; and He will deliver us out of your hand, O king. But even if He does not, let it be known to you, O king, that we are not going to serve your gods or worship the golden image that you have set up." (Dan. 3:13–18)

These young Jewish men looked into the face of a man who held all of the earthly power and refused to be intimidated. They knew the God who had given him that power. They refused to be intimidated. We have heard of the young women at Columbine who stared into the young eyes of evil and heard the question, "Do you believe in God?"

"Yes," came the answer.

"Then go and meet Him."

The last thing those girls saw was a blaze of fire. The next instant they saw Jesus as He took them into His arms. Dr. John Walvoord has observed that "sometimes it is not in the purpose of God to deliver his faithful ones from martyrdom."

Those girls at Columbine died for their faith. So did the students in Fort Worth and Paducah. We have known nothing of persecution in America. We have been on a two-hundred-year ride of religious freedom and liberty. But those days are over.

The Parable of Two Sky Divers

John Piper writes in his extraordinary book, *Future Grace*, of two sky divers:

Picture two skydivers. The are both free falling. Their speed is the same. They both seem to be free. They are not entangled in any cords. They are not restrained by any safety wires. They are free as birds—it seems. But there is one crucial difference: only one of them has a parachute. Does this change the sense of freedom that they enjoy? Yes. Both are free to fall with gravity, but only one of them is free not to. The other is a slave to gravity, and gravity will kill him in the end. If he can somehow deny that he has no parachute he might be able to have an exhilarating experience. But if he realizes he is doomed, he will be enslaved through fear during his entire fall, and all the joy of this so-called freedom will vanish. He must either deny the reality (which will mean slavery to illusion), or succumb to fear (which will mean slavery to terror), or be rescued by someone with a parachute. So it is in this world.[3]

Piper is referring to Hebrews 2:14–15: "Since then the children share in flesh and blood, [Christ] Himself likewise also partook of the same, that through death He might render powerless him who had the power of death, that is, the devil; and might deliver those who *through fear of death were subject to slavery all their lives*" (emphasis mine).

When a believer truly understands the work that Christ accomplished on the cross. it sets him free from the fear of death.

Again to Piper:

So we are free from the fear of death. God has justified us. There is only future grace in front of us. Satan cannot overturn that decree. And God means for our ultimate safety to have immediate effect on our lives. He means for the happy ending to take away the slavery and fear of the present. If we do not need to fear our last and greatest enemy, death, then we do not need to fear anything. We can be free. Free for joy. Free for others.[4]

Shadrach, Meshach, and Abed-nego were free from the fear of death.

When Corrie ten Boom was a girl, her first realization of death came after a visit to the home of a neighbor who had died. It impressed her that someday her parents would die. Corrie's father comforted her. "Corrie, when you and I go to Amsterdam, when do I give you your ticket?" he asked.

Corrie answered, "Why, just before we get on the train."

"Exactly," responded her father, "and our wise Father in heaven knows exactly when we're going to need things too. Don't run out ahead of him, Corrie. When the time comes that some of us will have to die, you will look into your heart and find the strength that you need—just in time."

These young Jewish boys had been given what they needed in the hour of testing. And it enraged the king:

Then Nebuchadnezzar was filled with wrath, and his facial expression was altered toward Shadrach, Meshach and Abed-nego. He answered by giving orders to heat the furnace seven times more than it was usually heated.

And he commanded certain valiant warriors who were in his army to tie up Shadrach, Meshach and Abed-nego, in order to cast them into the furnace of blazing fire.

Then these men were tied up in their trousers, their coats, their caps and their other clothes, and were cast into the midst of the furnace of blazing fire. For this reason, because the king's command was urgent and the furnace had been made extremely hot, the flame of the fire slew those men who carried up Shadrach, Meshach and Abed-nego. But these three men, Shadrach, Meshach and Abed-nego, fell into the midst of the furnace of blazing fire still tied up. (Dan. 3:19–23)

Nebuchadnezzar had gotten used to all of the "yes"-men around him. When he ran into some "no"-men, he lost it. He became enraged and ordered the fire seven times hotter. This actually made very little sense. Geoffrey Kings tell us why:

And then he lost his temper. That is always the mark of a little man. His furnace was hot, but he himself got hotter! And when a man gets full of fury, he gets full of folly. There is no fool on earth like the man who has lost his temper. And Nebuchadnezzar did a stupid thing. He ought to have cooled the furnace seven times *less* if he had wanted to hurt them; but instead of that in his fury he heated it seven times *more*.[5]

The other stupid thing occurred earlier. Nebuchadnezzar had said, "What god is there who can deliver you out of my hands?" (Dan. 3:15). Now, he was not just challenging these three Hebrews; he was challenging their God. *He was about to find out who could deliver them from his hand!*

Then Nebuchadnezzar the king was astounded and stood up in haste; he responded and said to his high officials, "Was it not three men we cast bound into the midst of the fire?" They answered and said to the king, "Certainly, O king."

He answered and said, "Look! I see four men loosed and walking about in the midst of the fire without harm, and the appearance of the fourth is like a son of the gods!"

Then Nebuchadezzar came near to the door of the furnace of blazing fire; he responded and said, "Shadrach, Meshach and Abed-nego, come out, you servants of the Most High God, and come here!" Then Shadrach, Meshach and Abed-nego came out of the midst of the fire.

And the satraps, the prefects, the governors and the king's high officials gathered around and saw in regard to these men that the fire had no effect on the bodies of these men nor was the hair of their head singed, nor were their trousers damaged, nor had the smell of fire even come upon them. (Dan. 3:24–27)

What an absolutely amazing story! It still sends chills down my spine. I first heard it when my grandmother read it to me when I was about four or five. As a little boy I was amazed by this story.

There are many truths in this biblical account. But I want to single out the kernel that is at the center of the whole wondrous event. *They chose the fire.*

They went into the fire just as Wagner Dodge went into the fire. At some point you and I are going to face the fire. Maybe not the fire of death. But some kind of cultural heat will challenge us because of our faith in the one true God. And we will have to choose as well.

Living Sacrifices

Got problems? Is life hard and difficult? Come to Christ and He will take that all away!

Ever heard the gospel presented in terms like these?

Compare that invitation to Philippians 1:29: "For to you it has been granted for Christ's sake, not only to believe in Him, but also to suffer for His sake."

A grant is a gift. And this verse is telling us that Christians have been given two gifts: belief in Christ and suffering for Christ. Very few of us are told up front that in the Christian life we will suffer. But Paul was. When Paul met Christ on the Damascus Road and was blinded, Ananias was told to seek Paul out: "Go, for he is a chosen instrument of Mine, to bear My name before the Gentiles and kings and the sons of Israel; for I will show him how much he must suffer for My name's sake" (Acts 9:15).

Suffering is a gift? That's a gift I can do without! Actually you can't. You need it and so do I.

Have you ever heard someone say, "I'm grateful for all of the ease and prosperity that I've enjoyed, because it has deepened my walk with Christ"? I don't hear that too often. What I do hear goes something like this: "That was the most difficult and painful time of my entire life. But I wouldn't trade it for anything because of how much closer it brought me to the Lord."

There is a difference between suffering and persecution. Suffering is the normal hard stuff that happens to everyone. Migraines, tax audits, wayward children, poor health, problems at work, and so forth. But persecution is specific hardship and resentment coming your way because of your faith in Christ. That's the difference.

Suffering is a very valuable commodity. That's why there is so much of it in the body of Christ. I'll never forget meeting Ron and Peggy Roloff and their four kids, Ruth, Matt, Sam, and Josh, in 1983. They are one of the most remarkable families I have ever seen.

The three boys caught my attention. They were polite, well mannered, quietly self-confident, and obviously very happy and well adjusted. Oh, and there's one more thing. Matt, Sam, and Josh are dwarfs.

Ron and Peggy are average size, and so is Ruth.

But the three boys, against unbelievable odds, were each born with achondroplasia.

This family knows about suffering. Because of their assorted unique physical problems, Ron and Peggy have waited and prayed as their kids have gone through thirty major surgeries.

Matt Roloff is now a successful executive in Portland, Oregon. In his wonderful book, *Against Tall Odds*, Matt tells about one year that was the hardest of all. It began during Christmas of 1974. Matt and Sam were both at Shriner's Hospital in San Francisco. In those days the parents could only see their two boys two hours a week. In January, young Josh lapsed into a coma and was rushed to Stanford Hospital in Palo Alto, where he underwent emergency brain surgery. It was touch-and-go for seven weeks.

During this time, Ron would work ten to twelve hours on the night shift and then go directly to the hospital. He would try to catch an hour or two of sleep on a sofa before he went back to work. This went on night after night for weeks. During this time, Peggy's two young nephews drowned in a swimming-pool accident. And I failed to mention that Matt and Josh were in full-body casts.

Now here is the unbelievable part. When Josh was released from the hospital, the Roloffs could finally return home. But a short while later, Ron and Peggy found out about a Vietnamese family with eight children who had recently arrived in America. When Ron and Peggy heard of the suffering that this family had been through, they took them into their home because they felt so sorry for them for all they had been through.

The Roloffs have been tested by suffering. But may I also say that everyone who meets these wonderful people realizes there is something very precious in this family.

Suffering will test you.

Suffering will refine you.

Suffering will approve you.

And so will persecution.

Dying for Your Faith, Living for Your Faith

Persecution doesn't always mean death.

As a matter of fact, it usually means life.

Persecution is an intentional hostility (to use John Piper's term), either verbal, emotional, or physical, that comes upon us because we bear the name of Christ.

Persecution for most of us doesn't mean the fiery furnace or staring into the barrel of a semiautomatic pistol. Persecution is being passed over for a promotion. Persecution is being fired. Persecution is being snubbed or ridiculed. Persecution is being rejected by family members because of our love for Christ.

These are the kinds of persecution that most of us American Christians face. When you compare this to what most believers in the world are experiencing, it's child's play. It's very probable that in the coming days we are going to see the ante go up. So we can view these relatively easy times as training ground for what lies ahead.

Not that it's easy to have your family reject you. It isn't.

Not that it's comfortable to lose a job because you are a Christian. Right off the top of my head, I know of five very competent and capable Christians who were at the top of their respective professions. These five are the cream of the crop. And all of them were "let go" because of their faith. Now that wasn't the stated reason. But it was the reason. And everyone knew it.

These five individuals knew that their jobs were on the line. Each of them had kids in college. Those tuition bills are steep. They had a mortgage payment and all of the other expenses that go with raising a family. They knew what was on the line. They looked into the fire of their careers going down in flames. And each of them chose to step into the fire and take the heat.

Where are they now? None of them are making the salary that they used to make. Each of them has taken very significant financial hits. Three of the five have taken lower positions on the career ladder. One is in another field entirely, making half the money.

What they have in common is this: If they had to do it all over again, they would. Without hesitation. The had the honor of choosing to suffer for Christ's sake. Like Shadrach, Meshach, and Abed-nego, they chose to face the fire. Three things happen when you choose the fire:

Facing the fire tests you.

Facing the fire refines you.

Facing the fire approves you.

Suffering will test you and refine you and approve you. But suffering is something we don't choose. We don't choose cancer, migraines, or wayward kids.

But we can choose to face the fire.

There were other Hebrews with Shadrach, Meshach, and Abednego. They knew the truth. But they chose not to stand up for it. They couldn't take the heat.

Facing the Fire Tests You

Going through the fire tells us what we are made of. This is true not only of Christians, but it's also true of precious minerals:

> In this you greatly rejoice, even though now for a little while, if necessary, you have been distressed by various trials, that *the proof of your faith*, being more precious than gold which is perishable, even though *tested by fire*, may be found to result in praise and glory and honor at the revelation of Jesus Christ. (1 Peter 1:6–7, emphasis mine)

You have read 1 Peter 4:12 before, but it's worth another look: "Beloved, do not be surprised at the *fiery ordeal* among you, which comes upon you for your *testing*, as though some strange thing were happening to you" (emphasis mine).

The "fiery ordeal" they were going through was persecution. "Fiery ordeal" means, literally, "smelted in a furnace."[6] This concept is found throughout the Bible. And it is used of both silver and gold. Both of these valuable minerals come out of the mines with impurities. Those impurities are known as dross. The more pure the silver and gold, the more valuable.

Perhaps you have a nice piece of gold or silver jewelry. It took quite a process to get that to you. And it all started hundreds of feet below the ground:

> Out from the mine and the darkness,
> Out from the damp and the mold,
> Out from the fiery furnace,
> Cometh each grain of gold.
> Crushed into atoms and leveled
> Down to the humblest dust,
> With never a heart to pity,
> With never a hand to trust.
>
> Molten and hammered and beaten
> Seemeth it ne'er to be done.
> Oh, for such fiery trial,
> What hath the poor gold done?
> Oh, 'twere a mercy to leave it
> Down in the damp and the mold.
> If this is the glory of living,
> Then better to be dross than gold.
>
> Under the press of the roller,
> Into the jaws of the mint,
> Stamped with the emblem of freedom,
> With never a flaw or dint.
> Oh, what a joy the refining,
> Out of the damp and the mold,
> And stamped with the glorious image,
> Oh, beautiful coin of gold![7]

A gold coin is valuable because it has been tested. The impurities have been removed. Purity is what gives it value. There is only one test for silver and gold, and that is a fiery furnace. And so it is in the Christian life.

Persecution in any form is always a deep test. But it's for a reason that we go through these deep testings. It was Samuel Rutherford who said that when he was cast into the cellars of affliction, he remembered that the great King always kept His best wine there.[8]

Facing the Fire Refines You

"Lord, make me the person You want me to be."

Have you ever prayed something like this? If you have, you are going to face the fire. And you will go through the fire. It's called refining.

Brother Andrew knows about persecution. At great personal risk, for years he smuggled Bibles into Communist nations behind the Iron Curtain.

God will take away what hinders us if we mean business. If we say, "Lord, at any cost . . ."—and people should never pray that unless they truly want God to take them at their word—he will answer. Which is scary. But we have to go through the process. This is how it has worked in the Bible for the last two thousand years.

So we face potentially hard times, and we have to go through that . . . We play church and we play Christianity. And we aren't even aware that we are lukewarm . . . We should have to pay a price for our faith. Read 2 Timothy 3:12: "Indeed, all who want to live a godly life will be persecuted." The church has been much purified in countries where there was a lot of pressure . . . All I can say is be ready.[9]

Sobering words. But very true words. We haven't known much of the pressure of persecution in America. But those days are quickly changing. God is going to refine us through the pressure of persecution. No, everyone won't die for faith. But there is no question that we face uncomfortable situations more and more that will refine us. And that means choosing the fire.

In dealing with a rebellious Jerusalem, God describes the process of refining that He intends to take them through because of their unwillingness to obey Him: "I will turn My hand against you, and thoroughly purge away your dross, and take away all your alloy" (Isa. 1:25 NKJV).

God uses this same process in the lives of those who are walking with Him.

I appreciate Jim Cymbala's comments that I recently read in his and Dean Merrill's book *Fresh Fire*:

When the ore is brought to the surface, the work is far from over. The crushing, amalgamating, and smelting is still yet to be done. Silver does not melt until it reaches 960.5 degrees Celsius; only then does it start to yield up its impurities . . . [God] knows the absolute necessity of removing the dross from our silver, of heating us up to an uncomfortable point where he can, as the New Living Translation puts it, "skim off your slag" (Isaiah 1:25).

In the great heat of the fire, the slag rises to the top. The slag is accumulation of the impurities. And the refiner skims off the silver as the farmer's wife skims cream off the top of the milk . . .

[God] is absolutely ruthless in going after the things that spoil the flow of his grace and blessing into our lives. His process is to subtract in order to add. He will never make a treaty with our secret pockets of sin.[10]

When persecution comes, there are no treaties. When the fiery furnace of persecution is made seven times hotter, you have to decide who is Lord of your life. It's no time for compromise. You're either in or you're out.

Halfhearted Christians with secret sin never choose the fire. But it's the very thing they need to refine their hearts and get rid of the impurities that are holding them back.

Facing the Fire Will Approve You

Hebrews 11 is God's Hall of Faith. In that chapter we are introduced to the people of the Old Testament who walked by faith. And faith is the name of the game in the Christian life. "Without faith it is impossible to please Him" (Heb. 11:6).

We need to note verses 32–40 of Hebrews 11. They yield a surprising principle:

And what more shall I say? For time will fail me if I tell of Gideon, Barak, Samson, Jephthah, of David and Samuel and the prophets, who by faith conquered kingdoms, performed acts of righteousness, obtained promises, shut the mouths of lions, quenched the power of fire, escaped the edge of the sword, from weakness were made strong, became mighty in war, put foreign armies to flight.

Women received back their dead by resurrection; and others were tortured, not accepting their release, in order that they might obtain a better resurrection; and others experienced mockings and scourgings, yes, also chains and imprisonment.

They were stoned, they were sawn in two, they were tempted, they were put to death with the sword; they went about in sheepskins, in goatskins, being destitute, afflicted, ill-treated (men of whom the world was not worthy), wandering in deserts and mountains and caves and holes in the ground.

And all these, having gained *approval* through their faith, did not receive what was promised, because God had provided something better for us, so that apart from us they should not be made perfect. (emphasis mine)

The first half of this passage tells of those who did great exploits for God. You might say they were *prosperous*.

The second half of the passage tells us of those who suffered defeat and hardship for the kingdom of God. They were *persecuted*.

Here's the principle: There are two signs of God's approval. One is prosperity. The other is persecution.

The issue was their faith.

Some prospered because of their faith. Others were persecuted because of their faith.

We have experienced the first. And we are about to experience the second.

You may be thinking, *How did they go through such persecution? How did they handle the hardship?* God gave them grace. And when we face persecution—any kind of persecution—He will give us the same grace.

Jim Cymbala comes through for us one more time:

Does your theology include Jesus sitting on a refiner's stool, watching over a cauldron of liquid metal under which the fire is getting hotter and hotter? Can you see him reaching down with a flat ladle from time to time to skim off the impurities that have bubbled to the surface? Is our faith deep enough to yield to the refiner's fire?

Will we always be comfortable in this process? Of course not! Is it pleasant? Not at all. But it is our Savior's method of getting rid of the junk of our lives . . .

Do you know how the ancient refiner knew when he was finished, and the heat could finally be turned down? It was when he looked into the cauldron and saw his own reflection in the shining silver. As long as the image was muddy and rippled with flecks of slag, he knew he had to keep working. When his face finally showed clearly, the silver had been purified.[11]

And when it was purified, it was approved.

Nebuchadnezzar threw three men in the fire. But then he saw four men. The fourth was the Son of God. The Son of God who looked into the fire, saw His reflection in the lives of those three young Hebrews, and got into the fire with them. And when they saw Him, they knew they had been approved. It was worth facing the fire.

When we face the fire, let's choose as they did.

As He was with them, so He will be with us.

10

A FINAL WORD

The principal part of faith is patience.

—George MacDonald

THERE ARE TWO questions about coming judgment.

The first is "when?"

The second is "what?"

Let's take them in order.

When will this final devastating judgment actually come? No one knows. It could be a matter of months or a lengthy number of years. Undoubtedly, we all have our opinions on this issue, just as we do concerning the return of Christ. But when you get right down to it, only God knows when.

We have concluded from our study of Scripture that judgment will come. It is inevitable. But it may not be on our timetable. George Herbert said, "The mill of God grinds slow, but sure."

The apostle Peter penned these words under inspiration of the Holy Spirit:

But do not let this one fact escape your notice, beloved, that with the Lord one day is as a thousand years, and a thousand years as one day.

The Lord is not slow about His promise, as some count slowness, but is patient toward you, not wishing for any to perish but for all to come to repentance. (2 Peter 3:8–9)

This applies not only to God's timing in regard to the return of the Lord, but it applies to coming judgment. God has a plan. He has a timetable. And nothing can stop His plan from being implemented on time.

That brings us to the second question: What?

If judgment is coming, then what shall we do until it comes? Do we begin to make radical changes in our lives because judgment is coming? What in the world should you do?

You should probably continue to live your life just as you are living now. You should follow the direction that God has given you. You should continue to seek Him for guidance and leadership. And until He clearly gives you a new set of marching orders, you should stay the course.

It is not my responsibility to know when judgment is coming. It is my responsibility to know God, and Jesus Christ, whom He has sent. According to John 17:3, knowing God and Jesus Christ is eternal life. And if I have been regenerated by the Holy Spirit, then I possess eternal life right now.

God has a plan for my life and yours. Ephesians 2:10 makes that very clear: "For we are His workmanship, created in Christ Jesus for good works, which God prepared beforehand, that we should walk in them."

God has given us eternal life (Eph. 2:6–8), and He has designed something significant for each of us to do. As we seek Him and follow Him in obedience, He will direct us to accomplish the good works that He has designed for us to do. And those good works are not dependent on whether judgment comes or not. He prepared good works beforehand for Daniel, and He has prepared them for us.

What *is* important is that we remain teachable and obedient before Him.

Judgment will come on America, sooner or later.

But may I remind you that if you are part of the remnant, America isn't your home. Heaven is your home. We are here only temporarily. Quite frankly, we are exiles.

God told Habakkuk that judgment would come, and it did. Daniel went to Babylon in the first of three forced migrations. In Jeremiah 29, God addresses those Jewish exiles and tells them *what* to do:

> Thus says the LORD of hosts, the God of Israel, to all the exiles whom I have sent into exile from Jerusalem to Babylon,
>
> "Build houses and live in them; and plant gardens, and eat their produce. Take wives and become the fathers of sons and daughters, **and** takes wives for your sons and give your daughters to husbands, that they may bear sons and daughters; and multiply there and do not decrease.
>
> "And seek the welfare of the city where I have sent you into exile, and pray to the LORD on its behalf; for in its welfare you will have welfare." (Jer. 29:4–7)

In other words, God tells them to stay the course.

That's pretty good advice for the rest of us who are modern-day exiles.

A parallel to this advice can be found in the New Testament in 1 Thessalonians 4:10–12: "But we urge you, brethren, to excel still more, and to make it your ambition to lead a quiet life and attend to your own business and work with your hands, just as we commanded you; so that you may behave properly toward outsiders and not be in any need."

Paul tells them to attend to their own business: Work hard, be a good citizen, and take care of the needs of your family. That certainly fits what the exiles were told: Build houses, get married, have kids, and pray for the welfare of your town.

In other words, *be faithful to what God has called you to do; where He has called you to be.*

> Is your place a small place?
> Tend it with care—He set you there.
> Is your place a large place?
> Guard it with care—He set you there.
> Whatever your place, it is
> Not yours alone, but His
> Who set you there.
>
> —*John Oxenham*[1]

God called us to be faithful to the responsibilities of our lives in the place where He has set us.

But that's not all.

God had something else to say to those exiles: "'For I know the plans that I have for you,' declares the LORD, 'plans for welfare and not for calamity to give you a future and a hope'" (Jer. 29:11).

These exiles were living in the midst of judgment. The Lord told them that they would serve seventy years in Babylon before returning to Jerusalem. Good, loving fathers let their children know the terms of their punishment. That's what the Lord did here. But He didn't stop there.

He let them know that they had a future and a hope. They weren't to live in depression or misery. God had plans for them. And His plans are always the best plans.

Are you part of the remnant? Does God have your heart? Is your desire to walk with Him in obedience? Do you count on His mercy and forgiveness when you miss the mark?

Then He has plans for you. Plans for the welfare of your family and you. He has a future for you that He has custom-designed for you. He has ordained good works for you, works that He prepared before eternity, that you might walk in them and fulfill them.

You just need to show up every day, be faithful, and be obedient.

You've got a future.

You've got hope.

All because you've got Him.

Or, to be more precise, He's got you.

And He's got you forever.

Appendix

DEUTERONOMY 28

NOW IT SHALL come to pass, if you diligently obey the voice of the LORD your God, to observe carefully all His commandments which I command you today, that the LORD your God will set you high above all nations of the earth. And all these blessings shall come upon you and overtake you, because you obey the voice of the LORD your God: Blessed *shall* you *be* in the city, and blessed *shall* you *be* in the country. Blessed *shall be* the fruit of your body, the produce of your ground and the increase of your herds, the increase of your cattle and the offspring of your flocks. Blessed *shall be* your basket and your kneading bowl. Blessed *shall* you *be* when you come in, and blessed *shall* you *be* when you go out.

The LORD will cause your enemies who rise against you to be defeated before your face; they shall come out against you one way and flee before you seven ways. The LORD will command the blessing on you in your storehouses and in all to which you set your hand, and He will bless you in the land which the LORD your God is giving you. The LORD will establish you as a holy people to Himself, just as He has sworn to you, if you keep the commandments of the LORD your God and walk in His ways. Then all peoples of the earth shall see that you are called by the name of the LORD, and they shall be afraid of you. And the LORD will grant you plenty of goods, in the fruit of your body, in the increase of your livestock, and in the produce of your ground, in the land of which the LORD swore to your fathers to give you. The LORD will open to you His good treasure, the heavens, to give the rain to your land in its season, and to bless all the work of your hand. You shall lend to many nations, but you shall not borrow. And the LORD will make you the head and not the tail; you shall be above only, and not be beneath, if you heed the commandments of the LORD your God, which I command you today, and are careful to observe *them*. So you shall not turn aside from any of the words which I command you this day, *to* the right or the left, to go after other gods to serve them.

But it shall come to pass, if you do not obey the voice of the LORD your God, to observe carefully all His commandments and His statutes which I command you today, that all these curses will come upon you and overtake you: Cursed *shall* you *be* in the city, and cursed *shall* you *be* in the country. Cursed *shall be* your basket and your kneading bowl. Cursed *shall be* the fruit of your body and the produce of your land, the increase of your cattle and the offspring of your flocks. Cursed *shall* you *be* when you come in, and cursed *shall* you *be* when you go out.

The LORD will send on you cursing, confusion, and rebuke in all that you set your hand to do, until you are destroyed and until you perish quickly, because of the wickedness of your doings in which you have forsaken Me. The LORD will make the plague cling to you until He has consumed you from the land which you are going to possess. The LORD will strike you with consumption, with fever, with inflammation, with severe burning fever, with the sword, with scorching, and with mildew; they shall pursue you until you perish.

And your heavens which *are* over your head shall be bronze, and the earth which is under you *shall be* iron. The LORD will change the rain of your land to powder and dust; from the heaven it shall come down on you until you are destroyed. The LORD will cause you to be defeated before your enemies; you shall go out one way against them and flee seven ways before them; and you shall become troublesome to all the kingdoms of the earth. Your carcasses shall be food for all the birds of the air and the beasts of the earth, and no one shall frighten *them* away. The LORD will strike you with the boils of Egypt, with tumors, with the scab, and with the itch, from which you cannot be healed. The LORD will strike you with madness and blindness and confusion of heart. And you shall grope at noonday, as a blind man gropes in darkness; you shall not prosper in your ways; you shall be only oppressed and plundered continually, and no one shall save *you*. You shall betroth a wife, but another man shall lie with her; you shall build a house, but you shall not dwell in it; you shall plant a vineyard, but shall not gather its grapes. Your ox *shall be* slaughtered before your eyes, but you shall not eat of it; your donkey *shall be* violently taken away from before you, and shall not be restored to you; your sheep *shall be* given to your enemies, and you shall have no one to rescue *them*. Your sons and your daughters *shall be* given to another people, and your eyes shall look and fail *with longing* for them all day long; and *there shall be* no strength in your hand. A nation whom you have not known shall eat the fruit of your land and the produce of your labor, and you shall be only oppressed and crushed continually. So you shall be driven mad because of the sight which your eyes see. The LORD will strike you in the knees and on the legs with severe boils which cannot be healed, and from the sole of your foot to the top of your head. The LORD will bring you and the king whom you set over you to a nation which neither you nor your fathers have known, and there you shall serve other gods—wood and stone. And you shall become an astonishment, a proverb, and a byword among all nations where the LORD will drive you. You shall carry much seed out to the field but gather little in, for the locust shall consume it. You shall plant vineyards and tend *them*, but you shall neither drink *of* the wine nor gather the *grapes*; for the worms shall eat them. You shall have olive trees throughout all your territory, but you shall not anoint *yourself* with the oil; for your olives shall drop off. You shall beget sons and daughters, but they shall not be yours; for they shall go into captivity. Locusts shall consume all your trees and the produce of your land. The alien who *is* among you shall rise higher and higher above you, and you shall come down lower and lower. He shall lend to you, but you shall not lend to him; he shall be the head, and you shall be the tail. Moreover all these curses shall come upon you and pursue and overtake you, until you are destroyed, because you did not obey the voice of the LORD your God, to keep His commandments and His statutes which He commanded you. And they shall be upon you for a sign and a wonder, and on your descendants forever.

Because you did not serve the LORD your God with joy and gladness of heart, for the abundance of everything, therefore you shall serve your enemies, whom the LORD will send against you, in hunger, in thirst, in nakedness, and in need of everything; and He will put a yoke of iron on your neck until He has destroyed you. The LORD will bring a nation against you from afar, from the end of the earth, *as swift* as the eagle flies, a nation whose language you will not understand, a nation of fierce countenance, which does not respect the elderly nor show favor to the young. And they shall eat the increase of your livestock and the produce of your land, until you are destroyed; they shall not leave you grain or new wine or oil, *or* the increase of your cattle or the offspring of your flocks, until they have destroyed you. They shall besiege you at all your gates until your high and fortified walls, in which you trust, come down throughout all your land; and they shall besiege you at all your gates throughout all your land which the LORD your God has given you. You shall eat the fruit of your own body, the flesh of your sons and your daughters whom the LORD your God has given you, in the siege and desperate straits in which your enemy shall distress you. The sensitive and very refined man among you will be hostile toward his brother, toward the wife of his bosom, and toward the rest of his children whom he leaves behind, so that he will not give any of them the flesh of his children whom he will eat, because he has nothing left in the siege and desperate straits in which your enemy shall distress you at all your gates. The tender and delicate woman among you, who would not venture to set the sole of her foot on the ground because of her delicateness and sensitivity, will refuse to the husband of her bosom, and to her son and her daughter, her placenta which comes out from between her feet and her children whom she bears; for she will eat them secretly for lack of everything in the siege and desperate straits in which your enemy shall distress you at all your gates.

If you do not carefully observe all the words of this law that are written in this book, that you may fear this glorious and awesome name, THE LORD YOUR GOD, then the LORD will bring upon you and your descendants extraordinary plagues—great and prolonged plagues—and serious and prolonged sicknesses. Moreover He will bring back on you all the diseases of Egypt, of which you were afraid, and they shall cling to you. Also every sickness and every plague, which *is* not written in this Book of the Law, will the

LORD bring upon you until you are destroyed. You shall be left few in number, whereas you were as the stars of heaven in multitude, because you would not obey the voice of the LORD your God. And it shall be, *that* just as the LORD rejoiced over you to do you good and multiply you, so the LORD will rejoice over you to destroy you and bring you to nothing; and you shall be plucked from off the land which you go to possess.

Then the LORD will scatter you among all peoples, from one end of the earth to the other, and there you shall serve other gods, which neither you nor your fathers have known—wood and stone. And among those nations you shall find no rest, nor shall the sole of your foot have a resting place; but there the LORD will give you a trembling heart, failing eyes, and anguish of soul. Your life shall hang in doubt before you; you shall fear day and night, and have no assurance of life. In the morning you shall say, "Oh, that it were evening!" And at evening you shall say, "Oh, that it were morning!" because of the fear which terrifies your heart, and because of the sight which your eyes see. And the LORD will take you back to Egypt in ships, by the way of which I said to you, "You shall never see it again." And there you shall be offered for sale to your enemies as male and female slaves, but no one will buy *you*.

—Deuteronomy 28 NKJV (emphasis mine)

NOTES

Chapter One
1. Henry Blackaby, cited by Intercessors for America, P.O. Box 4477, Leesburg, VA 20177, 1999.
2. Focus on the Family newsletter, Oct. 1999, 5.

Chapter Two
1. *John Owen*, cited by David Wilkerson, Times Square Church Pulpit Series, *Freedom from Fear*, Worldwide Challenge; P.O. Box 260; Lindale, TX 75771.
2. *John Owen*, cited by David Wilkerson, *America's Last Call* (Lindale, TX: Wilkerson Trust Publications, 1998), 82.
3. Peter Marshall and David Manuel, *The Light and the Glory* (Grand Rapids: Revell, 1977), 120.
4. *John Owen*, cited by David Wilkerson, Times Square Church Pulpit Series, *Freedom From Fear*.
5. Ibid
6. Ibid

Chapter Three
1. Matthew Levy and Mario Salvadori, *Why Buildings Fall Down* (New York: W. W. Norton and Co., 1992), 68–69.
2. Thomas Watson, *The Ten Commandments*.
3. Ibid.
4. Bill Bright and John N. Damoose, *Red Sky in the Morning* (Orlando: New Life Publications, 1998), 38.
5. Walvoord and Zuck, 1436.
6. Marshall and Manuel, *The Light and the Glory*, 46.
7. Ibid., 216
8. Ibid.
9. Ibid., 217.

10. Ibid., 218.

11. Ibid., 221.

12. Ibid., 221–22.

13. Ibid., 226.

14. Ibid., 227.

15. Ibid., 228.

16. Ibid.

17. Ibid., 229.

18. Ibid., 231.

19. Ibid., 234.

Chapter Four

1. Carl W. Wilson, *Man Is Not Enough* (Fayetteville, GA: Andragathia Books, 1998), 57.

2. Martin Lloyd-Jones, *The Puritans: Their Origins and Successors* (Carlisle, PA: Banner of Truth Trust, 1987), 1–2.

3. Wilkerson, *America's Last Call*, 12–13.

4. Cited by Robert Kuttner, "It's Just One Thing After Another," Available from <http://www.washingtonpost.com/wp-srv/WPlate/1999-08/13/...> (Oct. 10, 1999). Internet.

Chapter Five

1. Dr. Alan Axelrod and Charles Phillips, *What Everyone Should Know About the 20th Century* (Holbrook, MA: Adams Media, 1995), 83.

2. David Wilkerson, *God's Plan to Protect His People in the Coming Depression* (Lindale, TX: Wilkerson Trust Publications, 1998), 10–12.

3. Paul Johnson, *Modern Times* (New York: Harper Perennial, 1991), 226.

4. James Dale Davidson and Lord William Rees-Mogg, *The Great Reckoning* (New York: Touchstone, 1993), 269.

5. Ibid., 147

6. J. K. Galbraith, *Financial Times Library of Financial Classics*, Thursday, July 29, 1999, Part I, 15, extracted from *The Great Crash of 1929* (New York: Penguin Books, 1954).

7. Ibid., 1, emphasis mine.

8. Edward Robb Ellis, *A Nation in Torment* (New York: Kodansha International, 1995), 28.

9. Galbraith, *Financial Times*, 21.

10. Ibid., part I, 5 (emphasis mine).

11. Ibid., 7.

12. Ibid., 11 (emphasis mine).

13. Ibid., 7 (emphasis mine).

14. Ibid., 38.

15. Ibid.

16. Charles Mackey, cited by Jerry Tuma, *Cornerstone Report.* Vol. 15, Number 6, 22 September 1999, 1.

17. Donald L. Cassidy, *When the Dow Breaks* (New York: McGraw Hill, 1999), 18–19 (emphasis mine).

18. Davidson and Rees-Mogg, *The Great Reckoning,* 266.

19. *The Wall Street Underground,* vol. 4, no. 5, April/May, 1999, 8.

20. Larry Burkett, "A Financial Riddle," *Christian Financial Concepts,* Issue 257, June 1999, 1 (emphasis mine).

21. "Is There No Tomorrow?," *World Magazine,* 7 August 1999, 14–15.

Chapter Six

1. J. I. Packer, *Knowing God* (Downer's Grove, IL: InterVarsity Press, 1973), 69.

2. D. Martyn Lloyd-Jones, *Faith, Tried and Triumphant* (Grand Rapids: Baker, 1953), 20.

3. Martin Lloyd-Jones, *God the Father, God the Son* (Wheaton, IL: Crossway, 1996), 81 (emphasis mine).

4. Malcolm McDow and Alvin L. Reid, *Firefall* (Nashville: Broadman & Holman, 1997), 279.

5. "Mission to Mars," *National Geographic,* November 1988, 747–48.

6. Walter Kaiser, Lloyd J. Ogilvie, general editor, *Mastering the Old Testament,* vol. 21, *Micah, Nahum, Habakkuk, Zephaniah, Haggai, Zechariah, Malachi* (Dallas: Word, 1992), 162.

7. Ibid., 162.

Chapter Seven

1. Bruce Wilkinson and Larry Libby, *Talk Thru Bible Personalities* (Portland, OR: Multnomah, 1983), 148.

2. H. C. Leupold, *Exposition of Daniel.*

3. Wilkinson and Libby, *Talk Thru Bible Personalities,* 150.

4. Bright and Damoose, *Red Sky in the Morning,* 61.

5. Ibid., 18.

6. Warren Bennis, *Old Dogs, New Tricks* (Provo, UT: Executive Excellence, 1999), 20.

7. Ibid., 25.
8. *The Book of Wisdom* (Sisters, OR: Multnomah, 1997), 13.

Chapter Eight

1. John Piper, *Future Grace* (Portland, OR: Multnomah, 1995), 295.
2. *God's Little Devotional Book for Leaders* (Tulsa, OK: Honor Books, 1997), 85.
3. Geoffrey Perret, cited by Brian Lamb, *Booknotes: Life Stories* (New York: Times Books, 1999), 110.
4. Cited by Alice Gray, *Stories for a Couple's Heart* (Sisters, OR: Multnomah, 1998).

Chapter Nine

1. Michael Useem, *The Leadership Moment* (New York: Times Business, 1998), 50.
2. Ibid., 51.
3. Piper, *Future Grace*, 356.
4. Ibid.
5. Geoffrey Kings, John Walvoord, *Daniel: The Key to Prophetic Revelation* (Chicago: Moody, 1971), 89–90.
6. J. Vernon McGee, *Thru the Bible*, vol. V (Nashville: Thomas Nelson, 1983), 708.
7. Ibid.
8. John Piper, *Desiring God*, expanded tenth-anniversary edition (Sisters, OR: Multnomah, 1996), 222.
9. Ibid., 237.
10. Jim Cymbala and Dean Merrill, *Fresh Fire* (Grand Rapids, MI: Zondervan, 1999), 179, 181, 183.
11. Ibid., 183.

Chapter Ten

1. John Oxenham, cited by Edy the Draper, *Draper's Book of Quotations for the Christian World* (Wheaton, IL: Tyndale House, 1992), 208.

ABOUT THE AUTHOR

STEVE FARRAR IS one of the most innovative and effective Christian communicatiors in the country. He speaks to thousands of men each year at Promise Keepers and his Men's Leadership Conferences, which are specifically designed to equip men to be more effective spiritual leaders in their homes, churches, and communities.

He is the founder of Men's Leadership Ministries and is a best-selling author whose books include *Point Man: How a Man Can Lead His Family*, which has sold more than 300,000 copies; *Standing Tall: How a Man Can Protect His Family*; *Finishing Strong: Finding the Power to Go the Distance*; and *Anchor Man*.

Farrar is a graduate of California State University, Fullerton, and Western Seminary in Portland, Oregon. He also holds an earned doctorate from Dallas Theological Seminary. He and his wife, Mary, reside in Dallas, Texas, with their three children.

STEVE FARRAR
In Person
In Your City